# African Geopolitics

# African
# Geopolitics

## Philippe Hugon

Translated from French by Steven Rendall

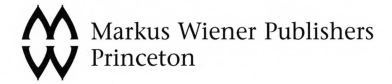

Markus Wiener Publishers
Princeton

This work, published as part of the program of aid for publication, received support from the French Ministry of Foreign Affairs and the Cultural Service of the French Embassy in the United States.

Cet ouvrage, publié dans le cadre du programme d'aide à la publication, bénéficie du soutien du Ministère des Affaires Etrangères et du Service Culturel de l'Ambassade de France représenté aux Etats-Unis.

The first French edition of this book was published in 2006; the second edition was published in 2007.

For information, write to:
Markus Wiener Publishers, 231 Nassau Street, Princeton, NJ 08542
www.markuswiener.com

Library of Congress Cataloging-in-Publication Data

Hugon, Philippe.
[Geopolitique de l'Afrique. English]
African Geopolitics/Philippe Hugon; translated from French by Steven Rendall.
Includes bibliographical references and index.
ISBN 978-1-55876-460-6 (hardcover : alk. paper)
ISBN 978-1-55876-461-3 (paperback : alk. paper)
1. Geopolitics—Africa, Sub-Saharan. 2. Africa, Sub-Saharan—Social conditions. 3. Africa, Sub-Saharan—Economic conditions. 4. Africa, Sub-Saharan—Foreign relations. I. Title.
DT352.8.H8413 2007
967—dc22
2007038086

Printed in the United States of America on acid-free paper.

*To my grandchildren,
who will see Africa
constructing itself*

# CONTENTS

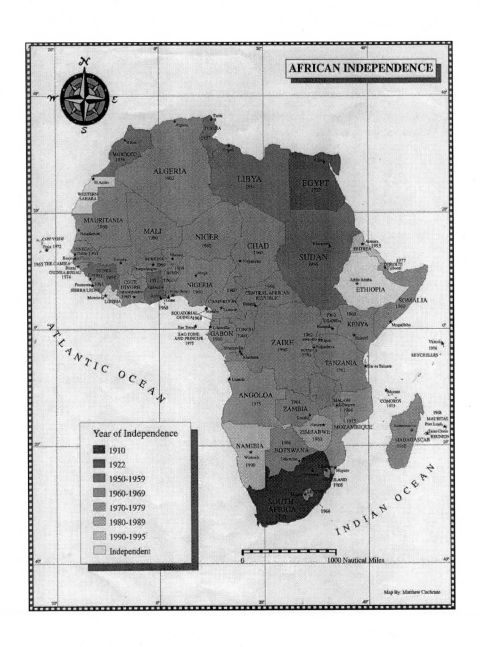

# Introduction

The term "geopolitics" is fashionable again, after a long period of being disparaged because of its connections with German imperialism. Strictly speaking, geopolitics is the study of the influence of geographical factors on politics. More broadly, it can be defined as the study of the forces at work in the field of politics. It is the art of international relations—the relations between nations, distinct collective entities that mutually acknowledge each others' right to exist. It concerns many non-state actors: territorial collectivities, multinational companies, organizations of international solidarity (OSI), churches, migrants, and diasporas all interacting in a transnational space. In the asymmetrical relations between Africa and the great powers, "hard power" —which expresses itself in coercion and force, especially military force—tends to be combined with a "soft power" that persuades through negotiation, propaganda, ideas, institutions, and the attractiveness of values and culture.

In works on geopolitics, Africa is now seldom discussed. However, during the period of direct colonialization, roughly 1870 to 1905, it was at the heart of the first debates on geopolitics and was used to illustrate the connections between territorial conquests, redrawn borders, and power relationships. Today, Africa appears as a whole to be peripheral to world strategic issues, even though within it there are many contrasts (Chapter 1). Economic, social, political, cultural, and symbolic issues are deeply intertwined at the same time that they are becoming independent of each other (Chapter 2). We see rapid change and broad internal challenges in African societies connected with the international scene (Chapter 3). Finally, since gaining independence, Africa has become a geopolitical actor in international relations and wants its voice to be heard (Chapter 4).

The process of drawing borders that allow inclusion and exclusion is always to some extent arbitrary. African countries bordering on the Mediterranean (etymologically, the sea surrounded by land) are generally seen as belonging to the Arab-Mediterranean cultural sphere. In this book, "Africa" will be limited to the forty-eight countries of sub-Saharan Africa, even though the continent includes North Africa, and even though many organizations, such as the African Union (AU), and numerous projects, such as the New Partnership for Africa's Development (NEPAD), are concerned with the continent as a whole.

CHAPTER I

# Between Marginality and Emergence: Contrasting Africas

Africa is part of the international system but is located on its periphery. The geopolitics of Africa is inseparable from the images, perspectives, and analyses that the social sciences have used in discussing it. It underwent profound changes between the pre-colonial and post-colonial periods and today is leading to different, contrasting Africas.

## Images and Ideas of Africa: A Geopolitics of Language

The origin of the term *Africa* is a matter of debate. It was first used to designate Ifriya (from the Berber word *ifri*, rocks) or the Romans' *Provincia Africa* (modern-day Tunisia), and was gradually extended to the Maghreb and then the whole of the continent. The expressions "Black Africa" and subsequently "Sub-Saharan Africa" have also been used.

The geopolitics of Africa begins with image and denomination, but also with conceptualization. The social sciences claim universal applicability, but they are also created in specific socio-historical contexts and problems may arise when their modes of analysis are transferred to different contexts. The meaning of Africa's past, marked by slavery and colonialism, is not the same for Africans and Europeans. Today, this disparity in memory corresponds to a territorial and historical fracture separating Europe from Africa.

## The discovery and images of Africa

The discovery of Africa by explorers, conquerors, merchants, and scholars began with its naming as the Other. Seven main archetypes have dominated the history of Africa's discovery:

1) The racist or evolutionary archetype of the barbarian, the inferior against whom one has to protect oneself or who must be civilized by importing the benefits of revealed religions, science, and institutions;

2) The paternalistic archetype of the child who has to be educated: Africa appears to be a continent that is lagging behind in humanity's evolution; the mother country must play an educative role with respect to this continent, which is not yet ready for democracy;

3) The exotic archetype of the noble savage, a "superior" living in communities that are marked by solidarity and harmony with nature and that must be preserved;

4) The humanistic archetype of the brother, a peer with whom we must cooperate;

5) The relativistic archetype of the foreigner who cannot be understood and whose difference ultimately leaves us indifferent;

6) The conscientious archetype of the slave in chains who must be freed from his master and his chains;

7) The solidaristic, compassionate archetype of the impoverished person who must be helped and whose development must be supported.

These archetypes are situated in a context. The images justifying colonial conquest have always led to resistance movements, whether humanistic[1] or utilitarian (liberal economists). The image of the noble savage or the brother prevailed in the philosophy of the eighteenth-century Enlightenment. The differentiation between savagery, barbarism, and civilization was dominant in the nineteenth century, particularly among the classical economists (Malthus), philosophers (Hegel), and historians, and in Marx's work written under the influence of Morgan's evolutionism (1877). Ethnologists tried to classify "races" or define ethnic groups. Durkheim's opposition between organic solidarity and mechanical solidarity, or Tonnies' contrast between community (*Gemeinschaft*) and society (*Gesellschaft*), whose chief point of reference is European, Greek, Latin, or German history, were generally adopted, as was the passage from family ties based on blood to national ties based on the soil and to the individual ties of Maine de Biran's social contract. The opposition between primitive mentality and rational mentality found in Lévy-Bruhl's early work (1922) was very influential. The image of the slave was dominant in liberation movements, and that of the brother in international charitable activities.

These images are part of a history of historical and mnemonic fracture repressing an ambiguous heritage. For purposes of administration, the colonial period was governed by classifications of races and tribes, frozen archetypes or stills stopping the film. In an essentialist and ahistorical view, the Other is pigeonholed and even biologized.

In contrast, the periods preceding and following colonialism are characterized by a re-appropriation of history, social and political processes, and modes of popular action. Works on political anthropology (Gluckman, Balandier) oppose the images disseminated by the media and the dominant images in terms of ethnic groups, compassion, or fear (images of migrants, starving children, soldiers, or victims of AIDS).

These images or iconographies are based on a naïve anthropology or a false consciousness (Cabel) that consists in reifying the Other and assigning immutable attributes. The linguistic battle refers us back to a geopolitics of assigning an identity to the Other as alien (native, tribe, ethnic group, solidarity, communities). A certain way of designating and looking upon the Other may be adopted by the Other and may shape his own self-image and behavior (cf. Sartre, Memmi, Mannoni).

Social science's images are at once ethnocentric and heterocentric. When we discover that the Earth is not the center of the universe, that there is no center, no east and no west, that one can write from top to bottom, from bottom to top, from left to right or right to left, we want to assign a meaning to these differences. So we reason in terms of progress (evolutionism), typologies (taxonomies), or signifying systems (systemism). A distanced analysis presupposes gradual approximations between a theory making universal claims and the particularities of specific areas and hybrid forms. It must avoid rashly transferring or transplanting concepts from other contexts. The discovery of the Other in its difference also functions as a magnifying glass showing us characteristics in an enlarged form and mirroring our own.

## The diversity of focuses and perspectives

Today, research on Africa is dominated by Afro-pessimism[2] or by an Afro-centrism that sees Africa's problems as proceeding from the outside, from the slave trade through colonization to the current tragedies.

How can we move beyond clichés that swing back and forth between an Africa that is underdeveloped, lagging behind, mired in age-old traditions, on the one hand, and, on the other, an Africa that is an exploited and alienated victim justifying the humanitarian, compassionate approach or the geopolitics of anti-colonialism (Chrétien, 2005)? How can we avoid the dualism that opposes tradition to modernity, individualism to communitarianism? "Ambiguous Africa" (Balandier) constructs its modernity along different avenues. It cannot be reduced to identity-based assignments in terms of tribes, ethnic groups, or communities. It is dangerous to idealize communities in the name of a so-called solidarity. It is important to locate the conflicts and power relationships that operate around common goods (Olivier de Sardan, 1995). Africa is not the sole victim of violence, which is the common lot of all human societies. We see in Africa a range of registers, norms, and rules. The referents are permeable, mixed, and hybridized. The tensions among them lead the actors to be involved in negotiations, ruses, compromises, crises, and violence.

Images of Africa also differ depending on the perspective adopted. A top-down approach shows that Africa is more a passive object than a geopolitical actor: on the international scene, it has lost its geopolitical importance and is more globalized than globalizing; it is placed in a long-term trend toward stagnation leading to marginalization with respect to international commercial and financial flows and to foreign debt that is difficult to manage. With 10 percent of the world's population, its share of the world's GDP is only 2 percent of world commerce and 2 percent of foreign direct investment. Its poverty indices are the highest in the world. Thirty-three of the forty-eight least advanced countries and thirty-six of the forty-five countries with weak indices of human development are in Africa. In Africa, 180 million people are undernourished, 25 million have AIDS. In 2005, seven countries were at war.

In a static, statistical representation, the listing of such indicators makes it possible to compare, rank, and classify Africa at the bottom of the international scale. However, everyone knows that what counts is rarely counted, and that statistics for poor countries are not very reliable.

By adopting a bottom-up approach and by shifting the point of view, the landscape becomes more varied, differences in relief appear, and "internal dynamics" (Balandier, 1971) emerge. Africa has become an actor on the international scene since independence and is becoming increasingly important on the demographic and cultural levels. Since independence, African countries have tripled in population and quintupled their urban population, while maintaining the borders of emerging nation-states. In two generations, they have undergone considerable cultural and structural transformations. In general, the population of the bush has moved toward the cities, where it has access to infrastructures, images, and new cultural references. Major institutional changes have been made—fiscal reforms, liberalization, and progress toward democracy. Actors at the bottom have been able to invent, innovate, and create activities that can help satisfy basic needs. Popular or "informal"

(Hugon et al., 1994) economies have constituted modes of accommodation, ingenuity, and life or survival for the masses. The development of infrastructures, educational and sanitary systems, and productive apparatuses and the emergence of educated elites and civil society make Africa in the twenty-first century very different from what it was in the immediate post-independence era. A process of democratization is underway and apartheid has disappeared.

Another focus seeks to move beyond appearances to reveal a deep Africa—the Africa of permanence, characterized by long-term persistence of values, a relationship to the sacred, social structures and rhythms that are out of synch with global time, the Africa of real powers and even of illicit activities organized around predatory economies and wars (Bayart et al., 1997).

## Geopolitical representations of Africa

Geopolitical representations are largely determined by international authorities and vary over time. The non-aligned movement (the Group of 77) and the north-south opposition, supported in particular by the United Nations Conference on Trade and Development (UNCTAD), promoted the unity of the south, the periphery, or the Third World (the 1955 Bandung Conference and Nkrumah's role). The Third World, emerging as the third-estate (Sauvy) or constituting a third path in addition to those of the Western powers and the Soviet Union, became largely an empty shell with the end of the bipolar confrontation and the East-West, North-South oppositions. Poor or less advanced African countries were trapped in poverty or were failed or failing states, fragile states, or even rogue states. New, regional powers such as South Africa emerged along with China, India, and Brazil to find a place in an international architecture constructed after World War II by the Western powers. Today, geopolitical language is governed by the international organizations in accordance with politically correct criteria and, beyond them, by the fact that English terms have been widely adopted (civil society, governance, party, poverty). The semiological battle also concerns information and disinformation disseminated by the national press that serves mainly as a relay for political forces.

Geopolitical representations are also forged in academic circles, chiefly occidental. The theories of imperialism, of regimes, of hegemony, and domination have been constructed in the West. The great paradigms distinguish "realists," who focus conflicts of interests among states; "liberals," who analyze market interdependencies and talk about developing countries; "solidarists," who emphasize cooperation and prefer the term "Third World"; "idealists" or "humanitarians," who emphasize assistance and repentance; and "dependentists," who contrast the center and the periphery (or peripheries) within the global capitalist system. An African approach gives priority to the African exception and seeks to deconstruct categories and elaborate a counter-discourse.

The reductive or essentialist state-centered or multi-centered oppositions that dominate the science of international relations must be put into perspective (Sindjoun, 2002). Thus, an international Africa *territorialized* around nation-states belonging to international society is opposed to a *reticular* Africa organized around transnational networks (firms, diasporas). Postmodern discourse on fragmentation, subversion, and the ruses of low-level actors contrasts with the discourse of nationalism or pan-

Africanism of the period when African countries were becoming independent.

Afro-centrism, which gives priority to Black African reality, confronts a representation of an Africa involved in globalization. There are, in fact, multiple configurations, and they are manifested in interactions between territory and networks, between international and transnational, between low-level actors and established powers. Dominated peoples and peripheral areas have powers of action and reaction. The categories of the social sciences must be used and at the same time contextualized, historicized, and put into perspective, and their vocabularies have to be decolonialized.

## From the Pre-Colonial to the Post-Colonial Period

The history of Africa does not begin with its discovery and colonization by Europeans. It varies extensively depending on the region and the period. The absence of written documents allows only a fragmentary restitution of its past. The history of long-term processes and practices in the pre-colonial and post-colonial periods (Coquery-Vidrovitch, 1989; Ilife, 1997; Ki Zerbo, 2003) demonstrates both the persistences and the ruptures in African societies on the level of values and representations, of spatial configuration, and of the role of community, family, and ethnic networks. The African periphery and Africans have experienced histories imposed on them, but they have also reinterpreted, appropriated, and endogenized them.

## A mosaic of peoples and political organizations

It has been estimated that in Africa there are 850 societies (Murdoch) speaking 1,500 languages. Africa has a rich political history: it has experimented with all forms of social and political organization from very centralized models to segmentary societies, from control over vast areas of the Sahel to control over small areas. African societies have experienced forms of the state or power, "a necessity through which any society succeeds in battling the entropy that threatens it with disorder" (Balandier, 1978). Nonetheless, there are more leaders than rulers.

According to Evans-Pritchard's classic distinction, segmentary societies without states (composed of homogeneous segments with minimal division of labor) differ from centralized systems. The political organization of the great empires of West Africa (Ghana in the eleventh century, Mali in the fourteenth, Songhai and Bornu in the sixteenth) was based on commerce with the Arab world; their expansion and decay were thus connected with the vicissitudes of trans-Saharan trade. Other empires were based more on tribute (the Wolof state in Senegal, the cities of Hausa in Nigeria and Merina in Madagascar). The term *empire* in fact usually refers to areas into which ethnic groups expanded rather than to an organized political space controlled by an *imperium*. "In Africa, borders precede the state, which in turn precedes the nation" (Pourtier, 2001). Pre-colonial states lacked borders. Only buffer areas or security belts separated the great empires. Power was an accumulation of social ties and goods—not only material goods (represented in livestock-raising societies by cattle), but also symbolic goods. History is marked by the violence of conquests, very unlike indul-

gent images of changeless village communities characterized by exchanges of gifts and solidarity.

## The discovery of Africa

*Triangular commerce*

During the mercantilist period, direct colonization of
Africa remained limited (except in the Cape Colony).
Commercial penetration was carried out through the establishment of trading posts, ports of call, and transfer points
in the interior. The Cape Colony (founded in 1652) was the
largest European colony on the continent; along with the
west coast of Africa, it constituted an important port of call
on the way to India. West Africa was little involved in commerce. Africa was caught between the domination of Islam
in the north, of Europe in the West, and of India and the
Arab world in the East (Amselle, M'Bokolo, 1986). A commercial triangle linked Europe with Africa as a purveyor of
slaves and with the Americas as a source of precious metals,
sugar, and spices.

*The slave trade*

In Africa, there were Saharan, eastern, and Atlantic slave
trades; there was also an intra-African slave trade (Unesco,
1999). The eastern (and later Arabo-Muslim) slave trade
began in the sixth century in the Sahara and East Africa. It
has been estimated that between 650 and 1920, some 17
million persons were involved (Pétré-Grenouilleau, 2005).
The European, Atlantic trade lasted three centuries and
involved, between 1450 and 1869, eleven million slaves. It

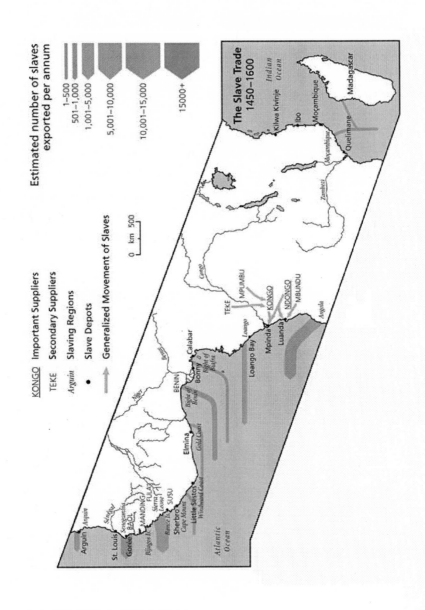

The Slave Trade
1450–1600

Estimated number of slaves
exported per annum

1–500
501–1,000
1,001–5,000
5,001–10,000
10,001–15,000
15000+

KONGO Important Suppliers
TEKE Secondary Suppliers
Arguin Slaving Regions
• Slave Depots
→ Generalized Movement of Slaves

0 km 500

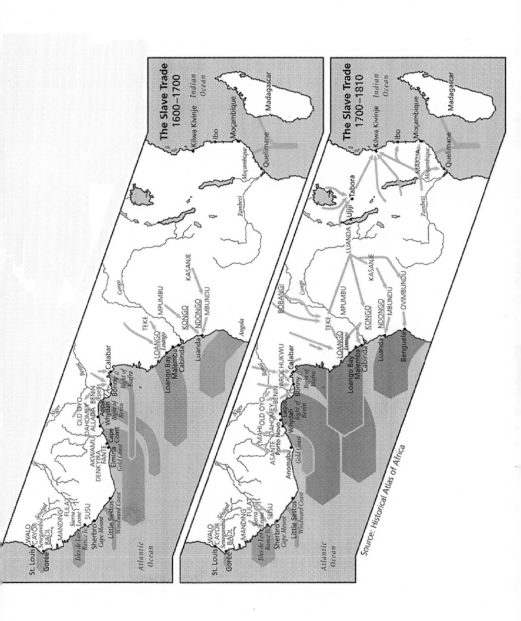

culminated in the late eighteenth century but did not officially disappear until the Congress of Vienna (1815). Slavery
itself was legally abolished only in 1848 in the French
colonies, in 1863 in the United States, and in 1888 in Brazil.
The eastern and Atlantic slave trades drew on African practices of taking slaves, whether the latter were captives taken
in war or for debts, people rounded up in raids, or black
farmers enslaved by nomadic tribes. According to Coquery-
Vidrovitch, one-fourth of the population of West Africa was
enslaved at the time of European colonization. Several
broker-states got rich on the slave trade: Ashanti, Benin,
Dahomey, and Oyo in West Africa and the kingdoms of
Congo, Matamba, Luanda, and Luba in Central Africa.

Understanding the cultural and political impact of the
trade in black slaves is essential. The memory of the
Saharan, eastern, and Atlantic trades is still alive among the
descendants of the people who were rounded up, like the
Yoruba in Benin, and many antagonisms and acts taken to
avenge the humiliations suffered are rooted in this history.
Direct colonization was justified by the slave trade. The
colonists often relied on former captives or dominated
groups. Certain practices of slavery continue in Mauritania
and Sudan.

The slave trade has recently been recognized as a crime
against humanity, and it is a major geopolitical factor producing frustration, bitterness, conflicts, and antagonistic
memories. Some people want Europe to repent or pay dam-
ages for the harm done, whereas many descendants of Afro-
American slaves also emphasize the responsibility of
Africans who were involved in rounding up slaves and in
the eastern trade. Still others point out that the trade
enriched Europe, that it participated in this "primitive accu-

mulation" (Marx), and that it helped Europe take off. This thesis has been strongly criticized, notably by Bairoch and by Pétré-Grenouilleau (2005). African slavery remains a major geopolitical factor because the accent is put more on the Atlantic trade than on the Saharan or eastern trades.

## Direct colonization (1870–1960)

*The European powers divide up Africa*

Colonization can be defined as the process through which a group takes control of a territory, occupies it, and exploits it by subjecting or eliminating its inhabitants. Colonial conquest leading to direct colonization began around 1870 and was ended by the Berlin Conference (15 November 1884–26 February 1885), which divided Africa up among the European great powers. It was financed by colonial parties and supported by military men and banks, whereas liberal economists and some humanists opposed it. It took different forms. The most extreme exploitation occurred in the Belgian Congo, which, under the control of Leopold II, was looted at considerable human cost.

Despite the technological power of the colonists' armies, their conquest confronted two main obstacles: problems of transportation in the Sahara and in the littoral areas, and, to the south, tropical diseases, especially malaria. The queen of Madagascar, Ranavalona I, said that malaria and the absence of roads provided her the best protection against the invaders.

The Berlin Conference did not really define borders but rather spheres of influence, so that the great powers could protect their private companies. Numerous treaties setting

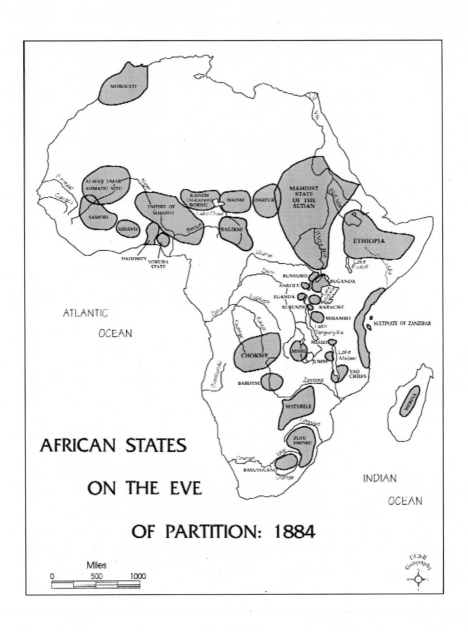

**AFRICAN STATES**

**ON THE EVE**

**OF PARTITION: 1884**

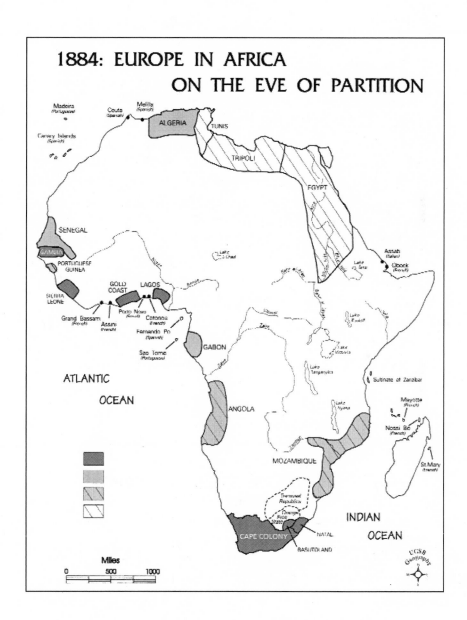

1884: EUROPE IN AFRICA
ON THE EVE OF PARTITION

territorial limits were subsequently signed. Then "a genuine race to actually occupy the territory began" (Brunel, 2004). Among the factors explaining this race were the search for external markets and access to raw materials, along with expansionist arguments connected with power. Borders were then defined in accordance with the European powers' spheres of influence. These borders were arbitrary in the sense that they were negotiated by the colonial powers, but they were not without foundation. From 1880 to 1895, the extent of French possessions in Africa increased from one million to nine and one-half million square kilometers. Contrary to views that interpret this as the expansion of a dominant capitalism, colonization was instead connected with the withdrawal to protected areas of Europeans and of threatened companies. It also had to do with nationalist, expansionist motives, a humanistic ideal, and the spread of a system of images. Africa was the last place where Europe could make territorial conquests. "Pacification" took diverse forms ranging from repression to negotiation.

## The colonial system

The colonial system had four general characteristics: the establishment of an administration in the form of indirect or direct rule; the appropriation of land; the domination of mercantile capital, which flourished at the expense of productive capital; and the establishment of a colonial pact between the home country and its colony.

The system involved levies more than development, revenue more than the accumulation of capital. The colonies were reservoirs of raw materials and outlets for manufactured products. However, beyond these characteristics, colo-

nial systems varied enormously depending on the colonizers and the societies colonized. Over time, they developed
considerably, leading foreign investment to dry up after
World War I. Subsequently, the economic crisis of 1929 led
European countries to fall back on their colonies and to
develop them. Only the period following World War II was
marked by a policy of development involving state capitalism and infrastructural projects.

The legacies of colonialism must be taken into account in
order to understand the current geopolitics of Africa. The
borders set by the colonizers were largely artificial, to be
sure, but they were considered unchangeable, and it was
independence that led to balkanization—particularly
through the breakdown of French East Africa and French
Equatorial Africa. Space was thus reconfigured on the basis
of the supremacy of littoral areas, ports, and connections
with Europe, and in relation to the location of capital cities.

Between 1880 and 1930, the population of Africa fell
from 200 million to 150 million because of forced labor,[3]
portage, disease, and genocides (three-quarters of the
Hereros in Namibia were exterminated). Population started
to rise again only after World War II.

Power structures were redefined, either by the emergence
of new elites that had earlier belonged to dominated groups
(the Hutu in Rwanda and Burundi, the Bantu of the Upper
Ubangui, the Ibo in Nigeria) or by alliances between chefferies and the colonial administrators. Cultural dispposses-
sion led to a change in language or in place names, but it
also provided access to international linguistic spheres and
resulted in a cross-fertilization that manifested capacities for
appropriation, trickery, resistance, hybridization, and rein-
terpretation. The colonial system, and especially the French

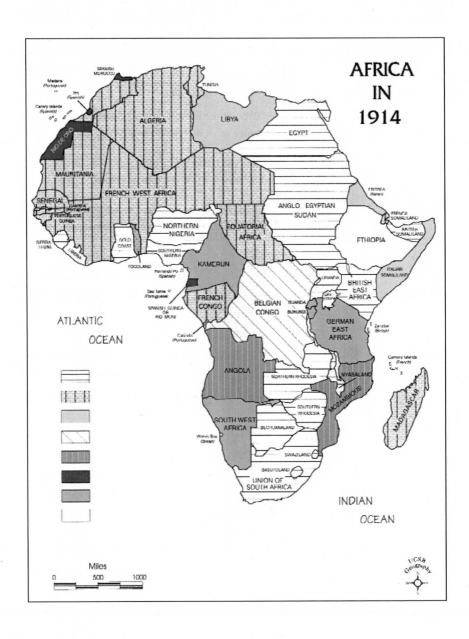

AFRICA
IN
1914

SPANISH MOROCCO
Madeira (Portuguese)
Ifni (Spanish)
Canary Islands (Spanish)
TUNISIA
ALGERIA
LIBYA
EGYPT
MAURITANIA
SENEGAL
GAMBIA (British)
PORTUGUESE GUINEA
FRENCH WEST AFRICA
ERITREA (Italian)
ANGLO EGYPTIAN SUDAN
FRENCH SOMALILAND
BRITISH SOMALILAND
SIERRA LEONE
LIBERIA
GOLD COAST
NORTHERN NIGERIA
SOUTHERN NIGERIA
TOGOLAND
EQUATORIAL AFRICA
ETHIOPIA
ITALIAN SOMALILAND
Fernando Po (Spanish)
Sao Tome (Portuguese)
SPANISH GUINEA OR RIO MUNI
KAMERUN
FRENCH CONGO
BELGIAN CONGO
RUANDA
BURUNDI
UGANDA
Lake Victoria
BRITISH EAST AFRICA
ATLANTIC
OCEAN
Cabinda (Portuguese)
GERMAN EAST AFRICA
Zanzibar (British)
ANGOLA
NORTHERN RHODESIA
NYASALAND
Comoro Islands (French)
MADAGASCAR
MOZAMBIQUE
SOUTHERN RHODESIA
SOUTH WEST AFRICA
BECHUANALAND
Walvis Bay (British)
SWAZILAND
BASUTOLAND
UNION OF SOUTH AFRICA
INDIAN
OCEAN

UCSB Geography

Miles
0    500    1000

colonial system, oscillated between differentiation, subjection, and assimilation.

*Political independence, or the post-colony*

Decolonization was only partly the result of movements of national liberation that were supported by powers like the USSR, the United States, Cuba, and the Arab countries. Decolonization resulted above all from an imperial overextension (Kennedy) and a cost-benefit analysis that revealed an increasing colonial burden.[4] Political independence made African states sovereign actors on the international scene, but it did not at first radically change the economic system. Africa was profoundly dependent economically, as is shown by its high degree of openness—to foreign influence and investments, for example; inadequately diversified exports; and a concentration of trade around the relationship with the former colonial power. Most energy products, intermediate goods and equipment, skilled labor, and training came from abroad. Foreign companies and governments were able to control the key banking, commercial, industrial, and transportation sectors.

The state, which had remained central to the economic system, was nevertheless generally weak. Africa experimented with different forms of government, including radical socialism. Nearly all countries established a single-party system. This post-colonial model gradually ran out of steam when preferential treatment began to end or states became less concerned with development than with pillaging their own countries' resources. Demographic and technological pressures helped exhaust the potential of an export model based on raw materials and the non-reproduction of ecosystems (shortening fallow periods, deforestation, etc.). The strategy of import-substitution was of limited validity in small countries where markets were in decline and liberalization dominated. The state performed its sovereign functions poorly, and in particular failed to provide adequate security.

## Contrasting Africas

Africa is a land of contrasts not only from a geographical and historical point of view, but also culturally, sociopolitically, and economically. The contrasts are all the greater because Africa is little integrated by language, by currency or markets, by the state, or by monotheistic religions. Huge in size (30 million square kilometers), young in terms of the age of its population or of the countries themselves, it is also the place where humanity originated and it bears the stamp of ancestral traditions going back to the earliest times.

These contrasts and ambiguities are all the more important because Africa is a site of spatial and cultural change, the contributions of successive civilizations being sometimes sedimented and sometimes fused. Janus-like, African masks have opposite faces. We can contrast gatherers and farmers with livestock raisers, sedentary peoples with nomads or migrants, peasants with city-dwellers, producers with merchants, people who live off the land with those who live off the sea.

### Typologies based on geographical criteria

Africa remains a continent far removed from the great international economic currents, in which the means and costs of transportation are factors producing isolation, economic marginalization, and weak internal integration. The commercial dynamics are related to open spaces (trans-Saharan caravans, commerce on the Red Sea, coastal areas). One of the crucial criteria from a geopolitical point of view is whether an area is an island, an enclave, or a coastal area. Some buffer states, such as Mauritania, Sudan, and Chad, participate in both the Arab and Black African spheres. With the exception of islands, the geopolitics of the sea is of little importance. Inadequate technological and financial resources make the geopolitics of the air equally insignificant. Several geographical criteria may be mentioned.

We can distinguish among a Sudano-Sahelian Africa, a humid and sub-humid West Africa, and a sub-humid and semi-arid Southern Africa. The Africa of "granaries" (millet and corn) differs from the Africa of "baskets" (tubers, planters in the forest), from herding areas, and from rice-growing areas. Two large, densely populated areas can be distinguished (Pourtier, 2001): West Africa between the Sahel and the Atlantic (200 million inhabitants) and, in the east, the highlands extending from Eritrea to Southern Africa. Between these two areas lies another, little-populated zone reaching from Sudan to Namibia and including the Congo basin. In areas of extremes, such as the Sahara or the Kalahari, desert conditions are dominant.

Five great regions can be differentiated: *West Africa* includes a zone of savanna (where Mande, Voltaic, and Songhaï are spoken) situated between the Sahara and the equatorial forest. *Central Africa* is organized around the River Congo and its tributaries, and its population speaks chiefly Bantu. *East Africa* includes the two oldest kingdoms in the south Sahara, Nubia (now Sudan) and Ethiopia, as

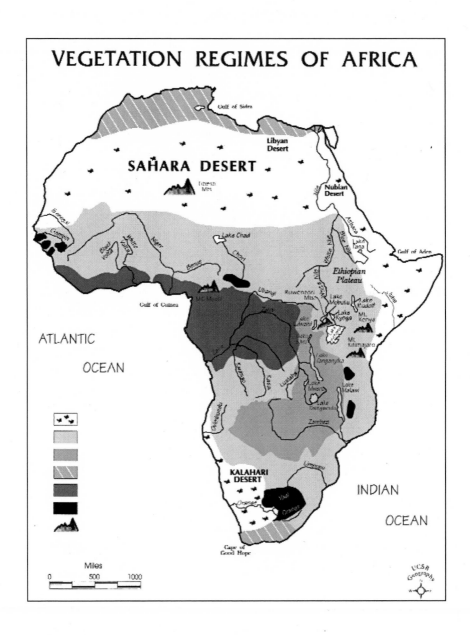

# VEGETATION REGIMES OF AFRICA

well as the Swahili-speaking world connected with the ocean. *Southern Africa* is peopled by groups speaking Koisan and Bantu and by Europeans, and it is dominated by South Africa. *The Indian Ocean islands* were more recently populated by Arabs, Indians, Indonesians, Europeans, and Africans.

## Plural trajectories

Several types of regional configurations can be distinguished:

*Countries at war, failed or fragile states*

More than 20 percent of Africans are affected by wars. The armed forces are in a lamentable condition because of their lack of equipment and supplies, the absence of esprit de corps, and collusion between private and political interest groups. There is widespread recruitment of child-soldiers and "sobels"—soldiers by day and rebels at night. Some states have become chaotic zones where warlords battle each other (Somalia, Chad, Sierra Leone, Sudan, Liberia) or the state does not have control over its territory (Côte d'Ivoire, Democratic Republic of the Congo) or over smuggling conducted by Mafias. Some disintegrating and anarchical societies no longer have mechanisms for regulating the economy or a government. They are, at best, under international supervision.

*Less advanced countries that are neither dependent on mining nor failed*

Less advanced countries are characterized by low income, inadequate human resources, and economic vulnerability.

Thirty-five African countries fall into this category. We will examine the case of the Sahelian enclaves.

The Sahel is a relatively homogeneous area from the point of view of climate, soil, demography, and social and economic organization. Peul and Arab-Berber nomadic herdsmen coexist with animist or Christianized farmers. On the whole, population groups are not very settled; urbanization has exploded. Agricultural exports are limited to peanuts and cotton; the latter is the main source of cash income for peasants, and it is a multiplying factor in rural areas. The Sahel has a very vulnerable economy and fragile systems. It suffers from the instabilities connected with climate (droughts), desert locusts, and international disturbances. For a long time, the effects of population growth have been associated with a degradation of ecosystems connected especially with the use of firewood. Foreign aid plays a crucial role in the Sahel. The regional dynamics of enclaves are connected with large-scale migrations toward coastal regions. There are also political and religious relationships with the Arab world.

*Countries dependent on mining and oil production*

The major economies based on mining are those of Guinea (bauxite), Liberia (diamonds), Mauritania (iron, oil), Niger (uranium, oil), Sierra Leone and Togo (phosphate), the Democratic Republic of the Congo (copper, columbite-tantalite), and Zambia (copper). The main oil-producing economies are those of Angola, the Congo, Gabon, Equatorial Guinea, Nigeria, Sudan, and Chad. These economies have specific dynamics centered on the creation and circulation of revenues and perks (the importance of the state, the domination of foreign multinationals, highly unstable receipts). Mining and oil conglomerates, which often compete with each other without any one of them controlling the market, are central to political power relationships and occasionally to conflicts. Resources are sometimes stolen (as in the Democratic Republic of the Congo), sometimes confiscated by a family clan (as in Gabon), and sometimes rigorously managed (as is the income from diamonds in Botswana). These economies' development depends mainly on the price of raw materials, the politics involved in providing secure access to the latter, and the strategies adopted by mining companies. They have a very dualistic structure. The mining sector, which generates state revenues and foreign currency, is the object of most investment and makes it possible to finance imports. Mining cities constitute either enclaves or distribution centers with macroeconomic and regional effects.. The rest of the economy is based on a precarious production apparatus and is strongly supported by a broadened system of redistribution. On average, mining revenues represent more than 90 percent of exports and more than half of state revenues. The importance of the tertiary sector and the weakness of agriculture are characteristic structural features. These economies have fallen victim to the "oil syndrome." Oil revenues should have led to a relaxation of financial constraints. In reality, their effects have been limited because of the importation of equipment and consumer goods, the repatriation of profits and salaries earned by foreign expatriates, and the flight of capital.

*Agricultural-export countries*

Several agricultural-export countries—notably Côte d'Ivoire, Kenya, Ghana, Uganda, and Cameroon—have experienced not only the exhaustion of the import-substitu-

tion model of industry, but also a process of capital accumulation,. The import-substitution model was based on pro-
tecting consumer-goods industries, drawing on foreign capital and managers, and a product market reserved for a west-
ernized elite. These countries based their development on
agricultural exports (coffee, tea, and cattle raising in Kenya;
cocoa, coffee, and palm oil in Côte d'Ivoire; cocoa and coffee in Cameroon). Thus, immediately after independence,
Côte d'Ivoire adopted a model of *state-regulated dependent
accumulation* based on immigrant labor (chiefly Mossis from
Burkina Faso), expatriate European managers, and the
influx of capital. The importation of these production factors, which was connected with the availability of land,
made it possible to specialize in agricultural exports and to
develop a dynamic modern industrial sector. This model is
in crisis because of the conjunction of depressed prices,
unmanageable foreign debt, and doubts concerning sociopolitical compromises and regional equilibria that are leading to political instability and conflicts.

## Open agro-industrial countries

Certain cases of *capital accumulation in an open economy*
that are connected with political stability can be noted,
especially in Southern Africa and the Indian Ocean
(Mauritius). Botswana, although it is an enclave dependent
on mining, has enjoyed strong growth because of effective
use of its natural resources (diamonds), the driving effects of
South Africa, which provides 80 percent of its imports, and
a liberal policy with regard to capital, combined with the
stabilization of export revenues. Mauritius is a case of an
economy that has used its specialty to improve its economy

by reinvesting its sugar revenues in a diversified productive system. Today it is suffering under the triple impact of the suppression of multi-fiber agreements, the sugar protocol, and the third oil crisis.

## Regional powers

Several regional powers are emerging: South Africa within Southern Africa, Nigeria within West Africa, and Ethiopia in the Horn of Africa. These states are pivotal for the great powers, particularly the United States, and are also the centers of regional hegemonies that are either real (South Africa) or potential and participate in the *pax africana*.

### South Africa

The Republic of South Africa, with 1.2 million square kilometers for 41.5 million inhabitants and a GDP of almost 200 billion dollars (2005), is the dominant power in sub-Saharan Africa. It represents 25 percent of the continent's GDP and 65 percent of the sales of the five hundred largest African companies. It accounts for 50 percent of salaried employees, half of the railway network, 40 percent of the highway network, and 50 percent of energy consumption in sub-Saharan Africa. The agricultural and livestock-raising sector, which involves 13 percent of the workforce, contributes 5.5 percent of the GDP and provides a self-sufficient food supply. The mining sector, with 8 percent of the workforce, contributes 10 percent of the GDP and 30 percent of the exports of nine main mineral raw materials worldwide. Manufacturing industries, which produce chiefly import-substitution goods, employ 16 percent of the workforce and provide 22 percent of the GDP. South Africa is also a military power (military spending rose to 2.65 billion dollars in 2004, or one third of the total in sub-Saharan Africa and 1.6 percent of the GDP). It sells weapons. A country that was long protected, where five conglomerates largely control the economy, and where the state has played a central role, South Africa has been undergoing a profound transformation since the end of apartheid (1989).

South Africa has enjoyed satisfactory economic and financial results, but the persistence of inequalities resulting from apartheid, the specter of unemployment (which affects 40 percent of the population), the brain drain, the burden of AIDS (25 percent of the population is HIV-positive), and violence continue to weigh heavily on this country. Disparities are still great. South Africa remains a mining economy that is caught between the gradual exhaustion of its reserves and the instability of prices for precious metals. The end of apartheid led to increased costs associated with the integration of the two communities. The main uncertainties concern centrifugal tendencies connected with regional disparities, an increase in unemployment among young blacks (40 percent of those with degrees), and white and mixed-raced people's fear of violence or affirmative action. How can the redistribution of power and wealth be reconciled with an efficient system of production and the external credibility necessary to realize the "African Renaissance" (Mbeki)?

South Africa remains a stable democracy endowed with a modern and progressive constitution and freedom of the press. It has been called a "mid-level power," a "pivotal state," a "regional hegemonic power," and "emergent." Its foreign policy agenda has been pragmatic since the end of apartheid. A first period of defending human rights and a second of pursuing commercial interests (Mandela) were followed by multilateralism within the South African Development Community (SADC), the African Union (AU), and the New Partnership for African Development (NEPAD). South Africa exercises its leadership in Southern Africa and beyond it, in sub-Saharan Africa, on the political, economic, and military levels. Soft power is winning out over hard power.

South Africa is expanding its sphere of influence through the AU, NEPAD, its military power, and diplomatic negotiations seeking to "find African solutions to African problems" (Mbeki). It is the integrating center of the South African Customs Union (SACU) and of the SADC and is substituting itself in part for the old colonial powers. South Africa has relations with forty-three African countries and largely controls the economies of countries in Southern Africa. On the other hand, it cannot be considered an economy that is converging with those of industrialized countries (low rate of growth, high risks, etc.)

*Nigeria*

Nigeria is the second most important sub-Saharan power. The sixth largest oil exporter in the world, a member of the Organization of Petroleum Exporting Countries (OPEC), a member of the Economic Community of West African States, (ECOWAS), a market of almost 100 billion dollars in 1980—but only 35 million dollars in 2005—Nigeria is the dominant economic power in West Africa. A federal state with more than 130 million inhabitants, it represents about one-sixth of the population, almost 20 percent of the GDP, and 40 percent of the foreign exchange of Black Africa as a whole. Its 2004 military expenses were 520 million dollars, or 1.2 percent of its GDP. It has great potential. It has major natural resources—in oil and natural gas, agriculture, hydraulic power, and mining (iron, columbite). The highway, banking, and commercial infrastructures are developed, and educational facilities have made it possible to train a well-qualified elite. Its oil revenues (2.5 million barrels per day) and gas revenues are estimated at more than sixteen billion dollars, and its foreign debt at 32.8 billion dollars. Oil and gas account for 95 percent of state revenues. This income is largely appropriated by military and political officials, whereas more than three-fourths of the population lives in great poverty. Nigeria remains a giant with clay feet; it has ethnic and regional differences, significant inequalities in income, and unstable petroleum resources. The economy is hampered by major bottlenecks such as a lack of managerial and technological competence, the influence of tribalism on the allocation of jobs, political criteria affecting the siting of industries, the clumsiness of the administrative apparatus, low levels of profitability in large projects (such as the Ajaokuta steel mill), and the inadequacy of electrical and telecommunication facilities and of secondary roads.

Nigerian society is fractured along various lines. The ethnic mosaic is organized around three major groups ("the Big Three"): Hausa and Peul Muslims in the north, Yoruba in the southwest, and Christianized Ibos in the east. Nigeria is diplomatically active and claims to speak for Africa. It includes within its sphere of influence the areas on its borders. It opposes France's presence within the Economic Community of West African States (ECOWAS), in which it seeks to be the hegemonic power. Nigeria's instability has always been an obstacle to the full use of its power.

*Ethiopia*

Ethiopia is located in the Horn of Africa, but lacks access to the ocean. It is a political center in its area and has a long tradition of self-government (although it was colonized by Italy from 1936 to 1941). It was Christianized in the fourth century, and in the nineteenth century it emerged as a Christian center in an Islamic or Animist Africa. Most of the people are Copts, but 40 percent are Muslims. The fall of Haile Selassie and the Menilek dynasty was followed by a Marxist regime that lasted twenty years, isolating Ethiopia and losing Eritrea and Tigray in 1988. The dominance of the Amhara group, the Abyssinian core of the centralized empire, has decreased since 1995 as a result of ethnic federalism. Ethiopia's economic potential is chiefly agricultural.

More than 700,000 people have died in the conflict with Eritrea, which has been independent since 1993. Ethiopia's military expenditures are more than 400 million dollars, or 4.3 percent of its GDP, whereas those of neighboring Eritrea are 154 million dollars, or 19.4 percent of its GDP. In 2007, Ethiopia invaded Somalia with the support of the United States.

# CHAPTER II

# Powers and Counter-Powers

## The Cultural Field

*There are some things that can be seen only with eyes that have wept.* —African proverb

### Between acculturation and a globalizing Africa in the cultural field

Soft power is exercised through symbols, images, values, norms, and rules. Africa participates in international society through its cultural powers and counter-powers. It is being globalized, but it is globalizing in the cultural domain. The cultural battle for Negritude, led notably by Léopold Senghor, has been a major factor in the affirmation of a black identity against the colonizers.

African cultures and civilizations are diverse. The nomads' traditions of hospitality and of exchanging gifts, the forest-dwelling gatherers' potlatch traditions, the Cameroonian Bamilekes' traditions of saving and investment, and the Sahelian great merchants' traditions of capital accumulation are all specific features that prevent us from generalizing. These civilizations are defined by their language, their technologies, their art, their religious beliefs, and their modes of economic, social, and political organization. Nonetheless, beyond the divergences there is a relative unity of cultures with oral traditions referring to a cosmogony.

African cultures continue to be shaped by orality and rurality. In rural societies, gifts that create ties are more important than goods that are transferred through commercial exchange. The emphasis put on fecundity and large families, the importance of gerontocracy and myths, the humiliations suffered and the victories magnified—all are transmitted from generation to generation: "An old man who dies is a library that burns" (Hampate Ba). The power of the magico-religious world is seen in diverse cultural manifestations. Thus African art is characterized by an aesthetic unity and a diversity of styles. It reproduces and at the same time transfigures rites and myths. The "artist" is an elite craftsman, often a blacksmith. More than a work of art, the object is loaded with symbolic meaning, and even with magical powers and vital forces. The initiatory experiences provided by cults involving possession by spirits renew the connections with ancestors and gods that control fecundity, fertility, and healing. Initiatory rites make it possible to discover the hidden and achieve mastery over the body.

Naturally, these cultural referents have been modified by the encounter with other referents connected with colonialization, urbanization, and globalization. The religions of orality have been altered by the religions of the book. Education has introduced a sense of causality, experimentation, and analysis as opposed to symbolic thought. The magico-religious world has not, however, been eliminated. Colonization sought to impose other systems of value, and from these arose a confrontation and a syncretism in the domains of language, religion, and norms. Cultural developments are connected with collisions between civilizations and cultures. Technological and industrial civilizations have tried to impose themselves by their technological and military superiority and their economic efficiency. The result is a process of *acculturation* connected with the contact, confrontation, and endogenization of different cultures and civilizations from which arises a cultural syncretism but also a rift between several referents. Africans have their feet in the Neolithic and their heads in the Internet. What is a virtue from the point of view of the community—polygamy, solidarity, respect for names and hierarchy—becomes a vice from that of efficiency and competitiveness (nepotism, clientelism, tribalism). African literature expresses this cultural ambivalence and ambiguity (Kane, *L'Aventure ambiguë*, 1961). Balandier (2003) speaks of Africa's cultural vitality—"*métissage*, mixture, and acculturation transform, connect, invent, and add"—whereas Ki Zerbo (2003) notes "the slow but sure erosion of African cultures."

Africa's culture—its literature (several Nobel prizes), music, design, and films—is influential and plays an important role in creating political awareness. The diasporas, cultural mixtures, and various emigrations are part of Africa's presence in the world. At the same time, Africa is connecting itself to the global system through new modes of telecommunication. Television networks and satellite transmission have become strategic stakes for great powers (Arab, American, European). Images and information are conveyed by mobile phones, television, and videocassettes; in cybercafes, the Internet provides access to the world of money, abundance, violence, and sex. "Moralism, violence and the ideal of material success thus constitute, in new syncretic forms, an explosive mixture that is taken in above all by those who have been excluded from growth, and first of all by the young, the Ninjas and Rambos of the Congo or Somalia" (Dubresson, Raison, 2003, p. 216). There are intergenerational conflicts. Urban youths are challenging gerontocratic structures and chefferies.

The place of women is obviously central to cultural creation, and their status differs depending on the culture. They play an important role in domestic food supply and reproduction. They do most of the work of providing firewood and water. "Women are our aqueduct," say the Dogon. At the same time, their social status is often inferior in various degrees (clitoridectomy, polygamy) and play political or social roles only in certain societies.

Sports also play a central role on the political and social levels. They create a sense of national unity (both Côte d'Ivoire and Cameroon, for instance, have famous national soccer teams) and of belonging to the African continent (The African Nations Cup is a continent-wide soccer competition). Sports relate to youth's aspirations (cf. the emblematic figure of George Weah, a former soccer star and a candidate for the presidency of Liberia in 2005). African athletes are emerging on the international scene. They participate in worldwide soccer competitions; South Africa will host the World Cup in 2010. African sports have become Africa's best ambassador.

## The linguistic mosaic and the plurality of values

Language is a way of representing the world and constructing a culture. With 1,500 languages, Africa has one of the largest linguistic patrimonies in the world (Sellier, 2005). Vernacular languages can be divided into large families: Cushitic, Chadian, Nilo-Saharan, Nigero-Congolese, Khoi-san, and Malgasy. Vehicular languages (lingua francas) are used for communications between peoples of different languages (Dyula and Hausa in West Africa, Swahili in East Africa, Lingala and Hibanga in Central Africa). European languages borrowed from colonizers—English, French, Portuguese, and Afrikaans—are used as vehicular languages both within the continent and outside of it. Languages are strategically important in participation in cultural areas and in certain groups' domination of the language of international communication and the ability to access scientific knowledge. Linguistic bonds are forged through the International Francophone Organization, to which twenty-five sub-Saharan African countries belong; through the British Commonwealth; and through the Community of Portuguese Language Countries. There are numerous pidgins and creoles.

Can we speak today of African values? Yes, on condition that they are analyzed as plural, evolving, and irreducible to stereotypes in terms of communitarianism, solidarity, traditions, or even primitiveness. To inquire into values is thus to think about the tension, confrontation, or contradiction between universalism and relativism, the transcendent and the immanent, the openness or closure of representations. We can consider (a) that there are universals in every culture and civilization that found fundamental rights, and that societies experience an internal debate between freedoms and totalitarianism; (b) that values are also contextualized, anchored in histories, and are expressed in rules and laws that are specific to the society concerned. They differ in

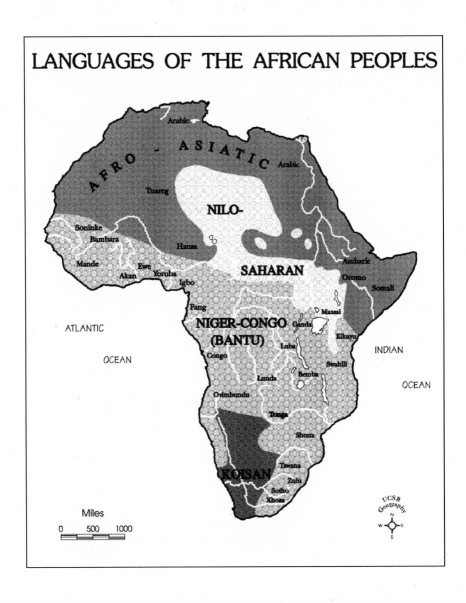

societies of the Mediterranean with a monotheistic heritage, in societies with animist traditions, in rural societies with a relationship to the sacred, and in urban societies that are more secularized (cf. clitoridectomy and polygamy, which are more important in rural areas); c) that values also express power relationships, conflicts, and impositions or persuasions carried out by dominant groups. They are often instrumentalized. Societies that are dominated, frustrated, or fascinated by values to which they cannot accede tend to fall back on fundamentalist values and enclose themselves in a rejection of difference; d) that at the same time, certain values founded in a given socio-historical context tend to be universalized because they are based on scientific knowledge (the earth is round and moves around the sun), and/or on battles for freedom (human rights, the struggle against slavery, indivisible civil, economic, social, or cultural rights). It is the multiplicity of heritages and intertwined, overlapping, and cross-border values that are the basis of fundamental values.

## The religious field

Religion, which is at the heart of geopolitics, plays an increasingly important role in Africa (*Esprit*, 2005). However, we must take into account the complexity of its relationship to politics, adopt a historical perspective, and avoid the type of Manicheanism associated with Samuel Huntington (and his thesis of the "clash of civilizations"). Religion cannot be reduced to private beliefs, nor can it be assimilated to a political process. It is not something imposed from outside but an appropriation and permanent re-creation. It is at the heart of representations and meaning. Religion is the cornerstone of every social, political, and economic institution. Among the Dogon, "people dance the system of the world," as the filmmaker J. Rouch put it.

## The different African religions

We can speak of *animist* religions, non-revealed religions, homeland religions, oral religions, or so-called "traditional" religions. They refer to an ancestral world and the transmission that is connected with it by founding a social order of reproduction. The ancient is a mediator between ancestors and the living and guarantees the society's harmony with the world of visible and invisible forces. The environment has a sacred character. The vision is eco-centered. These religions are undergoing a major revival, especially in urban areas. We can understand nothing about politics in Mali if we are not aware of the role played by sorcerers, or about Benin if we forget the role played by voodoo (almost two-thirds of the population believes in it). In traditional rural societies, the distinction between the profane and the sacred is erased: every economic or social activity is subject to a rite. Nature is expressed through the forces that animate it. Thus there is a close tie between man and nature that participates in the same vital force. Ancestors live in symbiosis with the living. Sacred time is linked to profane time. The depreciation of the future corresponds to the value placed on the beyond. Ultimately, people prefer to invest in a tomb rather than in material goods, because one dies for eternity and life is ephemeral. Becoming is perceived as a realization of the ancients' project.

Thus the secularized, material, economic act is secondary. The profane use of something matters less than its sacred use. The ambivalent time of traditional activities is given priority over productivist time. The gift and counter-gift are deferred exchanges of goods whose temporal periods and meaning to are opposed to relationships of equivalence in commercial exchange (cf. the Bilola among the Fangs, which is close to the Melanesian potlatch). Society is a system of symbolic relations and not a costly system of exchange.

Belief in sorcery provides a way of acting when misfortune strikes; it makes it possible to break intolerable relationships. In every society without a central political organization, the struggle for power is carried on through accusations of sorcery. The latter are also sanctions with regard to the non-respect of rules. In an eco-centered and not anthropo-centered conception, it is a question of respecting natural forces and not of mastering them. There is little or no distinction between the supernatural and the natural, the sacred and the profane: the religious universe is the sole order of things. Animals, plants, minerals, objects, the earth and the stars all participate in the same order of life, the same myths of origin, and the same vital force. The ancestors ensure the respect of disciplines, limits, codes of conduct, social cohesion, and hierarchy.

African *Islam* is very ancient. It is spreading in the Sudan and Sahel area and in East and even Central Africa, and concerns about 365 million Africans. It was brought to western Sudan in the eighth century by caravans and merchants and took root there. Islamization accelerated during the revival movement of the eighteenth and nineteenth centuries, and then when colonial administrations relied on Muslim social structures to supervise the population. African Islam is almost wholly Sunni. Today, one African in three is Muslim.

Simplifying, we can contrast an old Islam associated with marabouts and brotherhoods with a radical Islam associated with Arabizing Muslims. The brotherhoods always played an important role (Qadiriyya and Tijaniyya in nineteenth-century Mali, Murdiya in eighteenth-century Senegal, Sammaniya and Khatmiya in nineteenth-century Sudan). Since the 1990s, a certain radicalization of Islam functioning as an ideology and a strategy of power can be observed. *Sharia* is dominant in Sudan and northern Nigeria. *Jihad*, or holy war against evil, coexists with Black Islam's participation in a community of believers (*Umma al Islamiyy*that is supposed to be above states and individuals. Africa is experiencing or has experienced theocracies in Sudan, Mauritania, Somalia, Comoros, and Djibouti. Hardline Islam rejects the secularization of politics and does not separate the political sphere from the private sphere. It seeks not only to moralize society but also to change the state. It remains a minority movement and is not very compatible with a popular Islam full of syncretic beliefs and practices (Coulon in Coulon, Martin, 1991).

The implantation of Christianity, with the exception of the Ethiopian churches, dates from the missionary activity carried on by Portugal, which until 1843 enjoyed the privilege of the *padroado* (ecclesiastical patronage). In the nineteenth century we see a revival of missionary work by Protestants (connected with abolitionism and humanitarianism) and Catholics. Protestant missions were established in Freetown and in Cape, Livingstone's point of departure. The Catholic Society of Missions of Africa (White Fathers) was created in 1863. It could be said that the missionaries were agents of colonization by preceding or accompanying merchants and military men (the three M's). Missionaries often scorned old values and engaged in proselytism. Assimilationism was more pronounced among Catholics than among Protestants. In reality, relationships with the colonizers were often tense or conflictual. Colonial administrators often made use of Islam in their government, notably through indirect rule, which was extensively developed during the colonial period. In addition to their spiritual tasks, the missions were often involved in social and educational activities. The churches played an essential role in the training of nationalist elites. Since independence, there have been Africanization movements called "inculturation" (Catholics) or "contextualization" (Protestants). Today, Christianity is in full expansion in forested areas (West Africa, Equatorial Africa) as well as in Central, Eastern, and Southern Africa.

Independent churches, Ethiopian or messianic, play an important role (as did Kimbanguism in Zaïre). They are an indigenization or endogenization of imported beliefs.

*The rise of the power of religion and its connections
with politics*

The churches are forces of both resistance to and support for political powers that seek to instrumentalize them. The Christian churches contribute to sociopolitical compromises.[5] In failing states, the churches and religious networks serve as places of socialization, mutual aid in education and healthcare, and redistribution. They help relieve poverty. Religions are windows open on the world: through them come flows of money and information, and transnational networks are constituted (Dubresson, Raison, 2003).

Inversely, "political entrepreneurs" (Bayart, 1997) use the

religious register by creating cults or by taking over a church as an instrument of power. Some religions are developed in connection with the strategic interests of the Western powers and the Arab-Muslim world. Religious fundamentalism is growing, especially Pentecostalism associated with the United States and Islamism financed particularly by Saudi Arabia. The instrumentalization of religion is at the heart of conflicts in Sudan, Nigeria, between Eritrea and Ethiopia, and even in Côte d'Ivoire, where the "Muslim North" is opposed to a "Christian South."

## The field of the normative

*The plurality of legal orders*

Customary law is characterized by the complexity of its rules. Law regulates social life and serves as a principle of mutual coercion. Law alone can make different value systems compatible and transform them into effective social constraints. In Africa, institutional and juridical training are like geological formations in which strata of rules are sedimented and interlayered: customary or community laws, laws deriving from conquests (Islamic, Anglo-American, European), sui generis laws connected with independence, and laws issuing from conditions set by the Bretton Woods institutions or the European Union. Rules mark out paths, but there is more than one set of them and they are often violated. This plurality of references allows actors to play with the rules but it also makes them not very effective given the weakness of the judicial systems. Tensions between normative orders lead to negotiations, compromises, crises, and violence.

Subjective, economic, social, political, and cultural rights are emerging (rights to water, health, education). Almost all African countries have signed the Universal Declaration of Human Rights or the African Charter on Human and Peoples' Rights. These references may seem utopian when juxtaposed with *Realpolitik* and their minimal effectiveness. They are also avenues of recourse and show the urgent need for an independent and unbiased judiciary.

*Hegemonic powers and normative issues*

The hegemony of the great powers, and first of all the American superpower, is today exercised largely through normative supervision and the belief that development is connected with effective legal systems, the existence of a government of laws, and rules avoiding corruption and making economic agents secure. The economic school of property rights (North) emphasizes the superiority of certain organizational forms and the importance of respecting property rights and contracts. Depending on the path chosen by a society, arbitrary institutions can gradually become efficient. Other economists emphasize the diversity of norms, the plurality of laws depending on the society, the inadequacy of legal rules imposed by the dominant powers that do not include the actors' practices, and societies' contextual differences. The establishment of real property rights in Africa, which is supposed to make developers feel secure, leads to the exclusion of migrants, conflicts over real property, and instabilities that negatively affect the economic climate. The effectiveness of law depends on a level of economic development that makes the application of the laws possible (e.g., in the areas of child labor, food supply, or health).

We can see that rules are of strategic importance when we recognize the importance of the imposition of norms in taking over dominant positions. Some publications produced by the World Bank have tried to show the superiority of Anglo-American law based on individualism and common law over Romano-German or "legicentric" law. However, this superiority remains to be demonstrated for African countries because of the rarity of competent, unbiased judges and the role of precedents that are more difficult to apply than written codes. The hegemonic role of common law results from strategies connected with American lobbies within international organizations and with major law firms.

## The Social and Political Field

### The importance of familial communities

In African countries where capitalism and the state have not dominated the various spheres of society, family systems remain the matrix of societies. Unlike political networks, family networks were not destroyed by colonization. They differ greatly depending on whether they are based on matrilineal or patrilineal principles, blood ties, lineage or clan relations referring to a single real or fictitious ancestor, or types of marriage between lineages with rules of exogamy and dowry (Maquet, 1970). They establish solidarities but also the authority of the elders. The enlarged family based on lineage is the main site for the production of subsistence goods, procreation, and the labor pool. Intergenerational transfers and rights and obligations among younger and elder children partly make up for the absence of unemployment insurance and social protections. The family is often in crisis. Lineage structures, far from being dissolved in a modernity that can be assimilated to Western structures, seem to be growing stronger, but at the same time we see a process of individualization and exclusion. The redistributive crisis leads back to a redefinition of the rules of the social game. Against the background of an economic crisis, we observe a questioning of intergenerational relationships. Institutional hierarchies based on age are being modified. Solidarity in crisis is being replaced by a crisis in solidarity.

## Social networks and rapid restructuration

*Models of identity subject to evolution and negotiation*

The complexity of groups, peoples, and societies is obviously not reducible to "tribes" and "ethnic groups." These notions are historical constructs; they are transgressed by jokes, the plurality of patronyms, and nicknames. These labile identities are themselves subject to negotiation even if history has reified identities perceived as essential differences. Models of identity that establish social ties are not, however, reducible to citizenship or belonging to a nation. The public and private spheres are often combined or intertwined. Intergenerational solidarities and support for the unemployed, the pre-, non-, or post-productive are largely provided by private groups that people join voluntarily (tontines, associations, non-governmental organizations, mutual insurance arrangements) or to which they belong (lineages, ethnic groups, churches). These are all the more important because the agents are in a vulnerable, insecure situation, there are no relevant state institutions, the sense of citizenship is weak, and social policies have been changed by the economic crisis and by the adjustments required by the International Monetary Fund (IMF) and the World Bank.

## A structuration in multiple social groups

Structuration in social classes does not have the same meaning in Africa as it does in societies based on salaries. Salaried workers represent fewer than 10 percent of the active population and the working class fewer than 1 percent. It is difficult to speak of class consciousness among peasant groups. Many African societies are structured by strata, castes, or orders. The castes or groups based on status are characterized by endogamy; for example, among the Merina in Madagascar, the distinctions among Andriana (aristocrats), Hova (commoners), and Mainty (slaves). Among the Ankole we find relations of allegiance between lord and vassal substituting for the relationship between state and citizen. The Hutu and Tutsi in Burundi and Rwanda correspond to orders more than to ethnic groups. In Chad and Somalia clan membership is more important than ethnic membership.

Populations can be hierarchized from the "lowest of the low" to the "highest of the high": the rural and urban sub-proletariat, peasant groups, small urban producers, government employees, bureaucrats, and the dominant elites. The middle classes (salaried employees and government employees), whose salaries and guaranteed jobs have disappeared, are awaiting an illusory return of the old redistributive model. The uprooted, unofficial city-dwellers are seeing the abolishment of populist measures (for example, food subsidies). Young workers no longer have any hope of finding salaried positions.

At the societal level, we can distinguish among the classes (foreigners and national intermediaries) who control the economic capital, the intellectual elites who possess the educational capital (acquired in school) and who are often in conflict with inherited cultural capital, and the notables and bosses who have social and symbolic capital. Thus social struggles take place not only among *classes* (in the Marxist sense) but also among statuses or positions (for the holders of cultural capital), and also between races or ethnic groups that have social and symbolic capital. African powers are usually characterized by alliances with mercantile capital, notably with the Lebanese, Indo-Pakistani, and Chinese diasporas. There are African businessmen, merchants, and intermediaries who are generally very efficient. On the other hand, there are very few entrepreneurs, in Schumpeter's sense, who have long-term innovative strategies. Informal actors are more enterprising than they are entrepreneurs, more ingenious than they are engineers.

## A weak but emerging civil society

African civil society is embryonic but emerging. Labor and professional organizations are limited. Labor unions involve solely salaried employees, especially government employees. Multiple political parties have appeared. "The single party has lost its legitimacy as an organizational form capable of leading along the path to development. Even if it goes off track, the multi-party system leaves open a space for public debate" (Marchal, 2001).

Non-governmental organizations (NGOs) have emerged

as essential geopolitical actors. Burkina Faso has been called
"NGO Land." Outside, structured, voluntary interventions
are involved that seek to energize and inculcate social
change. The NGOs are situated between the market and the
state, between the private and the public. Their impact must
be studied in relation to the ability of local organizations to
persist and maintain themselves. They are economic organizations, intermediaries for aid that are part of a coordinat-
ing mechanism distinct from the market or the state. They
are based on solidarity and transnational citizenship.

At the international level, the rise of the NGOs and civil
society may be compared with the market and the state.
Adopting Polanyi's or Perroux's distinctions, we can differ-
entiate three typical representations of economies: the *commercial economy* based on the principle of exchange, private
interest, and the search for profitability or competitiveness;
the *public economy* based on services and redistribution, con-
straint, the search for the general interest, and authority;
the *economy of solidarity* based on reciprocity or cooperation,
the search for the common interest or good, and solidarity.

This triptych has to be refined because of the overlapping
borders of these three forms, the differences of scale that
they reflect, and their developing character. We see hybridizations involving the mutualization of private, public, and
associative resources and different kinds of partnerships.
The importance of each of these economies differs depending on the societies. Reconfiguring the economy and making it more complex lead to a radical modification of the
connections among the international *market economy*, the
*public economy* on the national level, and the *economy of solidarity* on the local level. The social and associative economy has taken on a global dimension with the organizations

of international solidarity and the emergence of a transnational citizenship.

The NGOs are playing an increasingly important role as counter-powers (movements proposing other visions of the world) in humanitarian aid, in the emergence of major questions and even the agendas for international negotiations, and in participatory democracy. Nonetheless, there is the question of their legitimacy and the limits of action undertaken on an emergency and/or uncoordinated basis. Humanitarian aid and emergencies have become markets for acquiring aid and objects of media attention at the expense of development (Brunel, 2004). Catastrophes, playing on compassion and humanitarian impulses, and emphasizing charity, must be related to the rise of economic liberalism and the failure of states to ensure security and equity.

## Rapid social changes

In a context of economic crisis or catastrophes such as wars or AIDS, it is important to take into account the acceleration of change. The latter concerns the growth of struggles over land, new actors such as unemployed people in school or urban property owners in rural areas, the growth of unofficial urban residence, and refugee camps. The result is new spatial structurations with the appearance of zones of transgression, border areas that escape the central government, and new regional centers as well as new political forces such as those of the churches, sects, and various membership groups. All this raises numerous questions. To what extent can redistributive systems come into play when the income passing through the government is reduced? How can solidarities be maintained in a context of the aggravation of social differentiations and inequalities of income? How can migrations play a regulating role when exclusive nationalisms are being exacerbated and private property rights established?

## Nation-states under construction:
## political power

The nation-state is a specific socio-historical configuration that is found only in a few African countries, even if it has acquired universality in the international architecture. Weak African governments are little connected with civil societies that are themselves emergent. Political powers have internal and external legitimacies. They depend on social hierarchies, the holders of economic power (e.g., merchants, foreign companies, Mafias), and symbolic power (religious powers, traditional chefferies).

There is not much of an institutionalized state, but there are multiple ways of practicing politics. In the pre-colonial period, there was differentiation but not discontinuity between segmentary and centralized systems. The colonial state was partly imposed as the transposition of a European model, but in reality the state apparatus was limited and had trouble "capturing" (Hyden) the population. The post-colonial state is a problem for coalitions in power and it is more often a place where classes are constituted than a reflection of those classes. It is sometimes called "imported" (Badie), extroverted, born of colonization, and manipulated from the outside. This thesis that the state is extraneous and cut off from civil society is extremely debatable (Dubresson, Raison, 2003).

*Different conceptions of African states*

• Differentiation and the historicity of the state

The elementary political relationship presupposes a division between the governor and the subject, whose roles are respectively to command and to obey on pain of coercion. Political systems are heterogeneous. Apolitical societies, that is, ones without relations between governors and governed, existed in hunter-gatherer civilizations, among some shepherds and farmers in the clearings of the rain forests in equatorial Africa and on the Gulf of Guinea. The conservative functions that are incumbent on political networks were fulfilled by family networks. At the opposite pole, state structures dominated the great empires and kingdoms. The chefferies or kingdoms had monarchical forms; power was personalized, the function of chief was sacred. States have functions of redistribution, directing collective affairs, providing internal security, and defending the group against external threats. On the whole, the religious and political domains coincide.

Colonization destroyed or subjected political networks, whereas family systems remained and continued to operate except in their societal function. Colonial government took over the functions of administration, justice, seeing to it that the law was obeyed and order maintained. The state had difficulty in capturing the populations and preventing "exit options" or trickery on their part.

During decolonization, leaders who had "evolved"—former university students, government employees, labor unionists, or military men—tried to create a state devoted to modernization and development. They usually sought to destroy the chefferies, emirates, and sultanates. They established a single party and developed ideologies ranging from African-style socialism to state capitalism. In most cases, these elites based themselves on groups to which they belonged or on clienteles. Student protests and military coups became common.

• The interdependency of politics and economics

Institutional structures of power can be analyzed from several points of view: from that of class interests, as a Marxist interpretation would assume; from that of the autonomy of the state apparatus, as realist political scientists would suppose; from that of the constitution of hegemonic blocs on the internal or international levels, or from that of utilitarian motives (the search for income), according to the school of public choices. In the *political economy of entanglements*, there is straddling between economic and political powers (systems involving politics with oil, cotton, or diamond producers), weak differentiation among the bureaucracy, the government, and economic interests, and collusive transactions (Banégas, 2003), the appropriation of wealth being both a way of financing the state and what it has at stake.

The state is not benevolent in the service of the common interest. It reflects interest groups that have seized power. It is often personalized and de facto identical with the holders of political power. In many African countries the *res publica* and private property are conflated (neo-patrimonialism), governments are being formed (sometimes by war, which is apparently a collapse of government), and there is a dichotomy between official, apparent structures and deep structures based on traditional powers or on the rise of new collective actors. "The rhizome state" (Bayart) acts like a tangle of networks serving to feed the system's continuation. In Africa, the state draws sustenance from the outside in order to feed its internal conflicts.

## Contrasting sociopolitical systems

Apart from sharing histories such as the slave trade and colonization, African sociopolitical systems are very different. On the whole, the state preceded the nation and the idea of citizenship is embryonic in comparison with the prevalence of community, clan, or regional bonds. In addition, we must distinguish among societies with ethnic cleavages, those that are characterized by clan membership (Somalia), segmentary societies without a state, and the ancient empires or nation-states (Ethiopia, Madagascar).

Many African governments function in a double register involving official structures that have an external legitimacy, on the one hand, and real structures that reflect sociopolitical compromises and accumulations of relational capital on the other. In most African societies access to power provides control over wealth rather than the other way around. Institutions are largely subverted by a personal patrimonial system based on external complicities. Lenders help reconstruct states, specializing in certain sectors (justice, police, army) at the expense of a coherent vision. Personal networks and solidarity win out over the institutionalization of the state. The post-colonial African state is usually characterized by a weakness leading to the near-collapse of institutions such as the army, and it is only tenuously connected with a barely-established civil society. The failure of the post-colonial model of the state and the depreciation of the state by liberal ideology have sometimes led to territorial fragmentation and the rising power of factions based on clan, community, ethnic, or religious membership.

It is obviously important to avoid any sort of generalization. A process of democratization is underway and institutional transitions, beginning with taxation, are progressing. Many states function normally, and several that have recently emerged from conflicts are reconstructing themselves (Burundi, Mozambique). However, we must also note the rapid propagation of sociopolitical crises that spread insidiously over borders and produce contagious effects. The reconstruction of states sometimes makes one think of Sisyphus.

• States are often overwhelmed

In theory, the state exercises its power over a territory delimited by borders. The structuring of this space is achieved through the creation of a network and the development of the territory. However, in Africa, the network is loose. The borders are contested and violated. The development of the territory is limited and often numerous regions escape state control (Igué, 1991).

A state that is overwhelmed cannot perform its ancient functions or provide its components, namely:

—the institutional structures of power, that is, a state that holds a monopoly on the use of legitimate violence in internal relations and is a sovereign actor on the international scene;

—the authority to negotiate and seek sociopolitical compromises (the state as arbiter, redistributor, regulator, facilitator, guarantor of the social bond);

—public activities that produce collective goods and services.

The neo-patrimonialist state (Médart, 1991) or rhizome state (Bayart) nourishes itself from the outside. The "politics of the belly" has been continual from the political control over mercantile capital accumulation taken by the great Sudano-Sahelian empires to the current nepotism and corruption. There are popular modes of political action that are helping to bring about the creation of a post-colonial state (Bayart in Coulon, Martin, 1991).

Corruption is a kind of behavior in which an individual deviates from the official norms and duties of elective or appointed public office for the purpose of enriching himself. It affects particularly extractive industries, public works, and bureaucracies, despite the numerous anti-corruption rules such as the Organization for Economic Cooperation and Development (OECD) convention signed in 2003, the African Union convention of 2003, or the United Nations convention of 2004. "Major" corruption can be distinguished from "minor" corruption, the latter being more a way of compensating for the decrease in revenues. In 2007 the NGO Transparency International classified Nigeria, Cameroon, Angola, Côte d'Ivoire, and Chad among the most corrupt countries in the world.

*States under adjustment and supervision*

Today, institutional reforms seek to create a legal space that can guarantee contracts, promote property rights, and allow "good governance." Privatization leads to the state's withdrawal from the productive sphere. Transfers of sovereignty appear at infra-national levels (decentralization) and supra-national levels (the role of the Bretton Woods institutions). Associations, NGOs, cooperatives, and the popular economy are playing a growing role as producers of collective goods and services. Nonetheless, the result has been less the establishment of a market economy than a recom position of economies that have remained dependent on revenues.

Democracy has become a necessary condition for politics. In addition to its diverse institutional forms, it is based on fundamental principles of freedom, the differentiation of public space from private space, a balance of powers, and the play of counter-powers. Like all human societies, African societies have historically had authoritarian dimensions with a role for the ancients, despots, and the play of democratic counter-powers. Colonization and independence have strengthened authoritarian regimes. Today, democracy is being imposed solely in the institutional form of electoral competition (multi-party system, free elections). Africa is certainly a continent that is ready for democracy, but the latter presupposes the emergence of counter-powers and especially an independent judiciary. Democratization is an endogenous process that inevitably entails struggles. "The public sphere is not solely an arrangement of the institutional sphere and civil society. It refers to political imagination" (Banégas, 2003).

These notions of governance that have invaded our vocabulary account for obvious realities of corruption, waste of resources, poor management of projects, and conflation of the public and the private that prevent aid from being effective. But they dissociate economics from politics and from policy or treat politics in managerial or economic terms and thereby ignore conflicts, contradictions and power relationships. The rule of law is supposed to play a central role in respecting contracts and establishing a stable environment.

Political regimes are classified by the NGO Freedom House according to how they deal with political rights and civil liberties: democracies, restricted democracies, constitutional monarchies, traditional monarchies, absolute monarchies, authoritarian regimes, totalitarian regimes, colonial dependencies, and protectorates. Tests connecting economic growth, political systems, political stability, and corruption yield inconclusive results. To be sure, corruption increases the costs of transactions, deforms the state's role in distribution and allocation, and favors tax evasion, but everything depends on how the money involved in corruption is assigned. North's claim (1990) that "Institutions are the main determinant of economies' long-term performance" is not confirmed.

## A precarious security system and failed or fragile states

"True public freedom can exist only when the security of individuals is assured," said Montesquieu. In many cases we can speak of states that have failed, are failing, or are fragile. The system of government or governmentality is unable to perform minimal sovereign functions, starting with providing security for individuals and property. A secure subject (individual or collective) is one that considers itself not threatened and has the means to respond to real or anticipated dangers. Security is a public good that is at risk because of the weakness or even disappearance of police forces, armies, and a judicial system that guarantees respect for civil and political rights.

Two types of armies were dominant at the time of independence: regular armies that had emerged from the old colonial armies and armies that had arisen from national liberation movements. The former were conceived in the colonizers' tradition and connected with the world wars. The latter were populist. During the Cold War, the sovereign function of providing security was often performed by the former colonial powers, notably with France's role as a policeman and defense agreements. Armies had increasing difficulties in fulfilling their role of providing security and maintaining the integrity of the national territory. The civilian powers feared military coups. They often declared their allegiance to non-legitimate powers. They were frequently behind in paying salaries and bills for equipment. Priority was given to maintaining internal order. African states, with the exception of South Africa, which sold weapons, have limited military potential on land, on sea, and in the air. The state has often privatized its defense (mercenaries, private militias), or even given warlords a free hand. The sovereign function of ensuring security is increasingly provided by international or regional forces.

Contrary to the liberal credo, societies can function in an efficient manner only if the state is strengthened in order to ensure security and create a favorable institutional environment, only if counter-powers avoid arbitrariness, only if businesses pursue long-term productive investment policies, and only if redistributive mechanisms function with regulated social tensions. Institutions and organizations are required as soon as the uncertain future has to be transformed into a project. The state as developer is a state that is a facilitator more than an achiever; except in the case of strategic options, it encourages more than it decides.

## The Economic Field

The African economy, whether it is analyzed in terms of commercial exchange, the production of material goods, or productive capital accumulation, has not achieved autonomy with respect to other social relationships. In its long-distance commerce, ancient Africa had an economy in the strict sense, and the great merchants of the Hausa cities were in no way inferior to those of Genoa or Venice at the time, though they lacked the latter's maritime capacities. But these circuits were not much connected with transactions at the local level. The latter took the form of mercantile exchange, reciprocity, allegiance, and redistribution/service.

Historically, of course, the sphere of the economy expanded. Merchandise developed through monetary taxation, forced labor, and the payment of dowries in cash. Nonetheless, even today a whole range of activities lies outside the market, and extraverted economic circuits are often enclaves. Many goods do not enter the sphere of economic transactions. Money is not a general equivalent with a liberating power over every kind of goods. Markets are limited to certain goods and do not concern all productive factors. The land is not very saleable. There is not much of a labor market. It is important to distinguish among the *domestic* sphere, the *market* as a place of monetarized exchange, and *capital*, or money used to accumulate money. Africa has

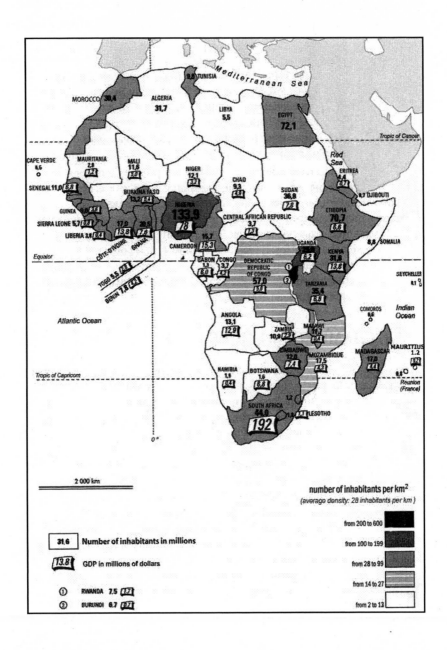

number of inhabitants per km²
*(average density: 28 inhabitants per km )*

**31.6**  Number of inhabitants in millions

*13.8*  GDP in millions of dollars

① RWANDA 7.5 *1.7*
② BURUNDI 6.7 *0.7*

from 200 to 600
from 100 to 199
from 28 to 99
from 14 to 27
from 2 to 13

experienced the first two levels. It has experienced and continues to experience primitive capital accumulation through violence, mercantile capital, but not productive capital (cf. Braudel, Bohanan, Dalton). Obviously we must avoid excessive generalizations, but the generic term "revenue economy" allows us to specify African economies in comparison with those of other continents.

## Economic dependency

Dependency reflects an asymmetrical position. It "does not mean predetermination by outside factors, but rather the unavailability of all the basic elements necessary for freedom of choice" (Balandier, 1966). In the long view of history, Africa has always been open to the world, thanks to efficient commercial networks based on gold, slaves, raw materials, or more or less illicit activities, depending on the period.

### Extraversion and marginalization

More than fifty years after gaining independence, African economies are not only exposed to fluctuations but remain centered on European economies that represent more than two-thirds of their areas of commercial exchange and their sources of capital. Africa has made few modifications in the structure of its exports: the primary raw material exported represented, in 1960 as in 2006, about half of all exports; exports of manufactured products constituted only 5 percent of the total. African economies are almost completely dependent for equipment and intermediary goods, and even for elementary, necessary consumer goods. Despite current reforms, most public revenues remain linked to customs duties. Dependency is heavy in matters of capital, foreign technologies, and expatriate skills. Only South Africa is a regional power with a relatively developed productive system.

*The erosion of preferential treatment and weak market power*

The logic of a revenue economy and weak gains in productivity lead to a permanent loss of competitiveness on the external market. This lack of competitiveness explains why it is difficult for firms or products to increase or even maintain their positions in the domestic and export markets. Africa's share in world commerce fell by more than half between 1970 and 2006. The exports of the countries of sub-Saharan Africa in 1970 constituted 3.1 percent of total world exports, but in 2007, they constituted only 2 percent (of which oil exports represented more than 40 percent). Experiencing a regressive specialization on basic products whose prices are mainly depressed, Africa is losing market share for its main agricultural exports: cocoa, palm, palm oil, peanuts, bananas, and rubber. It has maintained its market share only for coffee, sisal, tobacco, cotton, and tea. Africa is a price taker and not a price maker. Market power has shifted to the oligopolies, and the way added value is divided up can be explained largely by differences in consumers' purchasing power. Thus cocoa prices have long been very depressed and unstable, whereas the price of a chocolate bar in Europe is stable and even slightly increasing Côte d'Ivoire, even though it accounts for 45 percent of worldwide chocolate exports, lost market share at the beginning of the 1990s because of concentration and integration within the commercial chain controlled by Western industrial firms. In models of unequal exchange, the decrease in the terms of exchange and the unequal division of value was explained by asymmetrical divisions of the advances in productivity among countries with differing salaries. The current explanation is based on both the purchasing power of the Western consumer paying for brand-names and on the power of the oligopolies.

Many countries are still confronted by several problems that were already present when independence came (quasi-exclusive subordination with regard to exports of basic products, an embryonic industrial fabric, low rates of saving and investment, limited profitability of productive capital in view of the risk, limited coverage of health and educational needs, etc.), while at the same time having to manage the passive debt and respond to challenges both internal (notably population growth) and external (opening). After having benefited from the high prices for exports connected with colonialism and preferential commercial treatment, Africa is confronting the winds of competitiveness and participating very slightly in the international chain of value. African countries are dealing with the transition from administered, protected economies in the post-colonial manner to liberalized, open economies while suffering the erosion of preferential treatment and confronting globalization. With rare exceptions and despite internal reforms, African economies are still dominated by logics of revenue.

# A revenue economy with limited
# and unstable growth

Africa has remained largely a revenue economy in which it has not been possible to really launch the process of capital accumulation. Redistributive logics prevail over productive logics and the accumulation of social bonds has priority over that of goods.

## Factors explaining the economic stagnation

A large number of econometric studies explain the weak performance of African economies (Hugon, 2006). Many factors are suggested: ethnolinguistic fragmentation, geography (difficult communications, distance from the coasts, poor soil, diseases), history (insufficient specialization, the burden of colonization), politics (instability, insecurity, the costs of transactions, notably corruption), infrastructure (inadequate telecommunications, electricity, transportation, and public services), international conditions (exposure to outside shocks has increased because of economies' small size and their specialization in raw materials), and economic factors (low rates of investment are accompanied by a tendency to accumulate non-productive capital, distortions in favor of sectors that are not directly productive, weak demand, underdeveloped financial systems). The model of exporting basic products and import-substitution has not been able to launch a self-sustaining process leading to a diversification of production. Only a few countries, such as Mauritius and Botswana, provide notable examples of escape from this impoverishing specialization.

## TABLE 1
## The growth of sub-Saharan Africa's GDP
## (in percentage terms)

| | 1961–1973 | 1973–1980 | 1980–1990 | 1990–1999 | 2000–2005 |
|---|---|---|---|---|---|
| Population growth (annual) | 2.6 | 2.8 | 3.1 | 2.6 | 2.5 |
| Growth in GDP (annual) | 4.6 | 2.7 | 2.1 | 2.5 | 2.6 |
| Gross investment rate (percentage of GDP) | 15.0 | 20.6 | 16.0 | 16.0 | 17.5 |
| Private consumption | 72.0 | 66.0 | 68.0 | 69.0 | 69.0 |
| Public consumption | 11.0 | 13.0 | 15.0 | 16.0 | 15.0 |
| Exports | 22.0 | 26.0 | 29.0 | 28.0 | 26.0 |
| Imports | 19.0 | 25.0 | 28.0 | 30.0 | 27.0 |
| Gross domestic savings | 14.0 | 22.0 | 16.0 | 15.0 | 17.0 |
| **Total GDP** | **100.0** | **100.0** | **100.0** | **100.0** | **100.0** |

*Source:* Hugon (2006).

### The blockage of the system of production

Agriculture's low rate of productivity affects the economy as a whole. *Revenue agriculture* accounts for 30 percent of Africa's export income. For most states, it is the main source of para-fiscal revenue. *Subsistence agriculture* has made it possible to feed a population that is growing by more than 3 percent a year and an urban population growing at 5 to 7 percent a year. But it has developed mainly in extent. The *industrial sector*, in which natural resources are transformed and import-substitutes produced, has regressed after experiencing a long period of expansion between 1950 and 1980. The *tertiary or service sector* long retained the spirit of the slave-trade economy, despite liberalization. Its share is on the order of 40 percent of the GDP since independence, or significantly higher than the average in developing countries. The "sheltered" sector (where prices are not dependent on the world market) represents more than 50 percent of the GDP in oil-producing countries (commercial and noncommercial services). Sub-Saharan Africa is characterized by an inadequately developed, burdensome, largely extraverted financial system that gives priority to short-term loans and results in weak local financial networks in both urban and rural areas.

Parallel to the pressure of public expenditures, tax receipts have stagnated and public revenues connected with external commercial relations (customs duties on imports and exports, royalties, indirect taxes on imported products, tax evasion, and low tax bases) have dried up. The production of public goods and the state's performance of its sovereign functions are difficult to ensure.

*A strategic issue in the domain of mining and oil production*

The mining and energy sector represents two-thirds of sub-Saharan Africa's exports. In 2005, Africa consumed the equivalent of 150 million tons of oil and produced 200 million tons (including 104 million for Nigeria and 45 million for Angola).

Africa produces 10 percent of the world's oil and consumes 3 percent; it produces 8 percent of the world's natural gas and consumes 2 percent, or 13 percent and 10 percent of the world oil and gas exports, respectively. It has acquired a central position in the geopolitics of oil because of the technological revolution of offshore oil production and actors' need to diversify their sources of supply. It is becoming, especially for the United States, China, and India, a strategic issue. The place of hydrocarbons in trade between Africa and the rest of the world represents almost one third of African exports of raw materials, and thanks to technological advances, offshore oil production is developing. Oil nonetheless seems less a factor of development than a factor in the destructuration of societies and of waste generating perverse effects—the so-called "Dutch disease"—involving the appropriation of revenue by a limited group and even conflict. Extraverted enclaves function in wartime (diamonds in Liberia and Sierra Leone, oil in Angola). The resulting problems of governance and the deviations of petro-politics are acute, despite the existence of certain guardrails. Many indebted countries have mortgaged their resources and their hands are tied by the multinational oil companies.

## An "informalization" of the economy

Practices in an economic crisis lead to an informalization of African economies. The informal economy can be defined as a set of small-scale organizations in which there are few or no salaried employees, where little capital is advanced, but where nonetheless money circulates and goods and heavy labor are produced. The dominant rules are not salarial but customary, hierarchical, paternalistic. *Homo economicus* acts in accord with his interests; he is rational and relational, but in an uncertain context where constraints are relaxed (under-employment, abundant land, distance from the frontiers of efficiency).

As sites of innovation or adaptation, popular urban economies constitute ways of living and surviving for the greater part of the population. They make it possible to meet fundamental needs not covered by official systems: feeding, clothing, educating, and taking care of oneself, moving around or amusing oneself. The informal concerns feminine activities of supplying food (distribution, preparation, serving), providing personal and material services, and masculine activities of repairing, recuperating, and recycling industrial products, transportation, transformation, and fabrication.

On the one hand, small "informal" producers are inserted into networks characterized by interpersonal relationships of confidence and cooperation and connected with domestic units (non-dissociation of the domestic and productive budgets, use of family labor, distribution of surpluses within families). But on the other hand, they are inserted into the market and are subject to competition. Small units have very high birth and death rates. The informal economy reflects the resilience of societies with low productivity when faced with outside shocks. The informal economy also concerns integration into a parallel, Mafia-like international economy encouraged by the collapse of states and a world without law.

Historically, African countries have not much benefited from Europe's diffusion of a model of growth through the transfer of technology, direct investment, and an opening of European markets to industrial products that make a move up the scale possible. They have rarely been able to construct new comparative advantages or to master external openness through a combination of rigorous macroeconomic policies and selective industrial policies. The counter-examples are those of the integrated chain of cotton production in French-speaking Africa, which has increased its world market share from 4 percent in 1980 to 9 percent in 1990 and 16 percent in 1997, or Mauritius, which has moved up the scale and diversified its productive system and its international specialization.

Real and perceived risks, essential in determining the attractiveness of investments and in decision-makers' temporal horizons, are high. In 2005, according to COFACE, only Botswana had low risks, followed by South Africa, whereas the other countries were rated as mediocre (Gabon, Senegal), uncertain or dangerous (Cameroon, Côte d'Ivoire, Uganda, Zimbabwe), or even dreadful (Nigeria).

## A globalization undergone

The economic globalization of technology, information, and markets is accompanied by a strengthening of identities and a restriction of freedoms and human rights. The globalization of Africa is being undergone and imposed more than negotiated and mastered. On the international level, Africa has little financial and market power. It has a small share in world GDP, investment, commerce, stock-market capital, technology, or research. Governing officials have little room for maneuver in negotiating with transnational private economic powers but more diplomatic power, even if they can't play with the big boys.

*Globalization*

The term "globalization" refers to an interdependence among five processes: financial globalization, the global organization of production, the free circulation of merchandise, migrations and population movements, and the instantaneity of information transfer (Hugon in GEMDEV, 1999). It has favored certain emerging countries, notably in Southern and Eastern Asia (involving 2.3 billion people) and increased the marginalization and frustration of the African peripheries caught in the trap of poverty.

*Africa in globalization*

Despite their limits, we can use the indices of globalization to determine Africa's place in this process. These indices include:

—integration (exchange of goods and services, direct foreign investment and investment portfolios, revenues paid and received;

—social integration: personal contacts (telephone traffic, travel and tourism, transfers, migrations) and technologies (Internauts, Internet addresses, etc.);

—political integration (embassies, membership in international organizations).

According to these indices, Sub-Saharan Africa is relatively less globalized than the rest of the world, especially in the social domain.

### TABLE 2
### Indices of Africa's globalization

|  | Overall index | Economic | Political | Social |
|---|---|---|---|---|
| World | 2.46 | 3.31 | 3.08 | 1.24 |
| Sub-Saharan Africa | 1.51 | 2.21 | 2.16 | 0.40 |

*Source:* African Development Bank (2003, p. 185).

• Globalization and commercial marginalization

World commerce, two-thirds of which is carried out by multinational companies, is increasingly focused on products with high added value and on services, which are now included in WTO agreements. The dynamic comparative advantages are connected with technological innovation, the mobility of capital, and the distribution of new products. African countries play a small part in the chain of international value. A coffee or cocoa producer receives one-twentieth of the final value of the product sold on the markets of industrialized countries.

• Globalization and financial marginalization

World financial capitalism, which is dominated by stockholders, tends to prevail over managerial capitalism. Financial globalization is characterized by the interconnection of financial markets, an increase in new financial products, and financial crises. It results from deregulation, opening up, and the removal of intermediaries by securitization. Most capital available for financing development is now private. But Africa has limited access to international capital markets, and financial markets are virtually non-existent—with the exception of the Johannesburg exchange—despite the stock markets in Ghana and Nigeria and the regional securities market in Abidjan. Africa is not very attractive for private capital. Despite a recent rise, public development aid decreased after the fall of the Berlin Wall. Africa has been connected with the excess liquidity of the 1970s and the reversal in raw materials prices during the 1980s. Countries then borrowed funds to repay their debts. The latter had

often been contacted by corrupt governments and/or illegit-
imately. It had very negative consequences because of the
burden of servicing the public debt and because it led to
these countries being put under international supervision.
The ratio of debt to the GDP was more than 60 percent and
service on the debt was more than 13 percent in 2002. The
permanent indebtedness (200 billion dollars) changed
slightly because of measures taken under the Heavily Indebted Poor Countries initiative (HIPC) and multilateral
debt relief. These measures, which concern only a few countries, are not adequate to deal with the current challenges.

• The internationalization of production and the low attractiveness of direct foreign investments

In a world in which most international commerce, research and development, and innovation is provided by the
great multinational companies, the seductiveness of the
share of developing countries has become strategic. Foreign
sites intended for export activities presuppose logistics and
an economic, social, and technological fabric that cannot
be reduced to low salary costs and regulatory inducements.
With the exception of certain sectors such as oil or effects of
privatization in the agro-alimentary sector, telecommunications, water, electricity, distribution and transportation,
Africa attracts only 1 to 3 percent of global direct foreign
investment (10 to 30 billion dollars out of a total of 1,000
trillion dollars). The profits of American or European
branch operations certainly remain very high (on the order
of 28 percent in Africa), but the fact that these profits
remain in niches or in the development of natural resources
can be explained by the major risks run. Few firms engage

in sub-contracting for the purpose of exporting, despite the appearance of free trade zones (Mauritius and Madagascar). Except in major markets such as Nigeria or South Africa, import-substitution firms are suffering the effects of decreasing demand (the departure of expatriates, decrease in the income of the middle classes) and competition from contraband. Nevertheless, we see a diversification of investors in the context of liberalization and privatization. The low rates of direct foreign investment reflect a variety of factors such as the limited size of the economies and a pessimistic outlook on the growth of markets, institutional failures, and physical and social infrastructures, a weak economic and social fabric, and especially real or perceived risks, whether in terms of political instability, the volatility of political economies, or international instabilities.

• Information and communication and the digital and scientific break

Africa is suffering an exodus—indeed a pillaging—of competencies, and there is a major risk that a cognitive, digital, and scientific gap will develop. Education, which is central to the relationships among knowledge, abilities, and assets, is quantitatively and qualitatively insufficient to allow Africa to be in phase with the new economy of knowledge and cognitive capitalism. The drain of managerial talent has risen to 20,000 individuals a year and has to do with the push and pull of attractiveness for intellectually competent people. The scientific and technological gap leads to a centralization of knowledge around certain poles and a decapitalization of poor countries. We see growing divergences between educational systems at the international level between African countries caught in the trap of poverty and countries that have dynamic national systems for training and innovation. The impact of technological revolutions on Africa is very haphazard. Africa can benefit from decreasing prices (for computers, Internet access, mobile phones). New information and knowledge technologies have an impact on modes of learning, on firms' productivity and competitiveness (distance learning, the Worldspace project that uses satellites to broadcast digital radio programs). These revolutions are involved in strategies of penetration on the part of the great powers, notably the United States. Most of these networks are concentrated in the capital cities and concern only a limited segment of the population. A computer and its accessories represent seven to fifteen times the annual salary of the average African. In 2005, only fifteen African countries had access to the Internet outside the capital city and four countries had more than ten telephone lines per thousand inhabitants.

• Participation in a parallel world economy

Africa is also a place where capital is recycled, allowing money-laundering, the financing of foreign political parties, and overbillings, sources of private and public income. A *new triangular commerce* has been set up, linking Africa as an illegal exporter of raw materials to Western countries with Eastern countries that export weapons and mercenaries, while Eastern and Western countries are establishing parallel financial relationships with each other (Chataigner 2005). The expansion of the number of countries that have collapsed or are failing, rogue or pariah states, results largely from their participation in a criminal global economy.

The latter is manifested in the major corruption, arms dealing, money-laundering in offshore exchanges, and globalized networks for the sale of drugs, human organs, human beings, and sex. The illegal drug trade is estimated to represent 8 percent of world commerce and its annual sales at 400 billion dollars. The worldwide gross criminal product is estimated at 1.2 trillion dollars, corresponding to 15 percent of world trade. This parallel international economy is both a source of revenue and a factor in conflicts and the decomposition and composition of states. Traffic in diamonds, oil, and drugs has become a crucial source of wealth (Angola, Côte d'Ivoire, the countries of the Gulf of Guinea, the Democratic Republic of the Congo, Sierra Leone, Liberia, Guinea, Burkina Faso). Access to mining or oil deposits leads to overlaps between the positions of power and the positions of capital accumulation. Drug cultures are present in Lesotho, Côte d'Ivoire and Ghana. Senegal, Cape Verde and Mozambique are involved in transit trafficking. Drugs feed local crime and corrupt politics (Nigeria, Democratic Republic of the Congo, South Africa) as well as conflicts (Liberia, Sierra Leone, Casamance, Guinea-Bissau, Congo). Contraband and counterfeiting (Mauritius, Nigeria), flags of convenience (Liberia), tax paradises (Mauritius, Seychelles), and trafficking in wood (Central African Republic, Democratic Republic of the Congo) constitute some of the many sources for illegal economies.

# CHAPTER III

# Problems and Internal Challenges

Africa is characterized by a certain number of geopolitical problems that are internal to the continent and at the same time connected with the international environment by both their causes and their consequences, their prevention and their resolution. We will distinguish between peace and conflicts (section 1), the problems involved in sustainable development (section 2), and food supply problems (section 3).

## Problems of Peace and Security

Africa has become the continent where the number of victims of armed conflict is the highest in the world. With 13 million internal displaced persons and 3.5 million refugees, Africa's rate is twice that in Asia, whose population is five times greater (Commission for Africa, 2005). There are many kinds of conflicts. They differ in intensity, duration, and territorial extent. They may occur within a nation, between nations, or between regions. We can distinguish between civil wars and insurrections, armed conflicts and criminal violence, and conflicts between armed parties and terrorism.

To what extent do these forms of armed violence represent something new? Pre-colonial and colonial armed con-

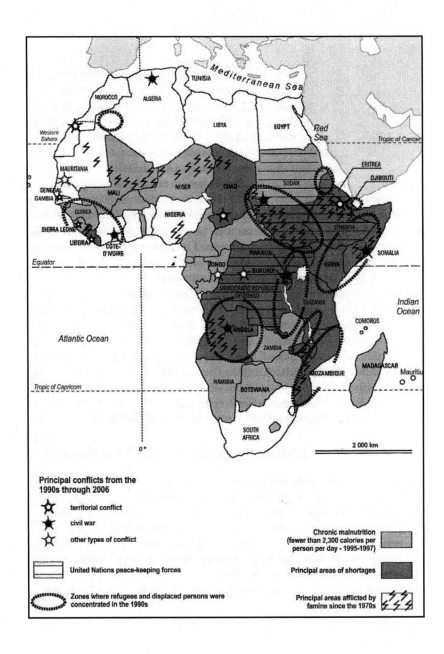

Principal conflicts from the
1990s through 2006

☆          territorial conflict

★          civil war

☆          other types of conflict

United Nations peace-keeping forces

Zones where refugees and displaced persons were
concentrated in the 1990s

Chronic malnutrition
(fewer than 2,300 calories per
person per day - 1995-1997)

Principal areas of shortages

Principal areas afflicted by
famine since the 1970s

flicts were a matter of conquering, plundering, and rounding up slaves. The wars of independence were linked to national liberation movements and the Cold War (Biafra, Eritrea, Ethiopia, Somalia, Angola, and Mozambique). Internal conflicts (civil wars, rebellions) are traditionally distinguished from external ones (international wars). This distinction has lost much of its pertinence since the fall of the Berlin Wall (Kaldor, 1999). African armed conflicts that are internal to the country are connected with regional and international networks. They cannot be treated, as realist theories suppose, in terms of nation-states pursuing power goals. We see a change in scale and intensity (Balancie, de La Grange, 2004). The conflicts of the Cold War period, which were characterized by ideological oppositions and the support of the great blocs, have been replaced by multiform guerrilla actions that are more intra-African and are accompanied by a partial withdrawal by the great powers (Clapham, 2000).

We may also ask what role is played by economic factors. African countries account for 7 percent of world military expenditures (7.1 billion dollars out of a total of 975 billion dollars total) and 26 percent of the major conflicts (five out of nineteen). Explained largely by exclusion and poverty, these conflicts are in turn factors contributing to insecurity and underdevelopment and reflecting vicious circles and the trap of poverty. According to some authors, ideological conflicts and old wars based on grievances have been replaced by conflicts that are more predatory and revenue-seeking and that are related to group identity (Collier, Hoeffler, 2000). This thesis regarding the novelty of these armed conflicts and the role played by economic factors is controversial. Critics claim that it is mistaken both in lumping together conflicts of different kinds and in seeing a rupture where there is a historical continuity.

## Armed conflicts and political economy

It is an illusion to believe that economics alone reduces violence and that free trade ensures peace. The *pax oeconomica* has been a *pax britannica* or *americana*. If all wars do not have economic motives, they all need to be financed. We can distinguish between closed war economies financed by local resources and economies of open war and guerrilla conflicts that benefit from outside financing and from political, military, and humanitarian sanctuaries (Ruffin, 1996). Generally, these categories overlap. Thus the National Union for the Complete Independence of Angola (União Nacional para la Independência Total de Angola, UNITA) relied on military support by Namibia, and had access to humanitarian sanctuaries and financing based on diamonds and even oil.

War and peace both have costs and advantages. We can assume that conflicts result from economically rational behavior on part of representative agents in an institutionally deficient context (Collier, Hoeffler, 2000). Empirical tests using normalized statistics show that countries with high per capita income, sufficient natural resources, a high degree of ethnic fragmentation, and low population have a very low risk of war, whereas countries with low per capita income, relatively few natural resources, a population divided into two large groups, and a large population are almost certain to face civil wars.

African economies are still largely revenue economies. Wealth is acquired more by appropriation than by creation.

The primary factors leading to war in Africa are the natural resources that make it possible to finance wars and are at the same time one of their main stakes. Thus we can distinguish between wars connected with oil revenues (Angola, Congo, Central African Republic, Sudan), diamonds (Angola, Liberia, Sierra Leone, Democratic Republic of the Congo), precious metals (gold and columbite-tantalite at Bunia in the Democratic Republic of the Congo), narcotics, land (Burundi, Côte d'Ivoire, Darfur, Rwanda), or control over water (people living on the banks of the Nile) or forest resources.

These conflicts occur in the context of state failures. They are rarely between states (the fighting between Ethiopia and Eritrea is an exception). Either they are between regions (north and south: Côte d'Ivoire, Uganda, Sudan) or they involve societies that have fallen apart or imploded (Democratic Republic of the Congo, Liberia, Sierra Leone, Somalia). Victory may not be desirable in order to divide up the revenues. War makes it possible to justify actions that would be considered crimes in peacetime. The economic advantages expected to result from civil wars are plunder, protection money, profits connected with the sale of arms, food, and narcotics, the exploitation of labor (taking slaves), control of land, theft of foreign aid, and the advantages of fighters living off their foes. These conflicts for the illegal securing of revenues cannot be reduced to predatory rebels alone. They can be caused by waste on the part of illegitimate governments or international private oligopolies. Guerrillas, rebels, and disaffected soldiers live on outside support, theft of products or foreign aid, and appropriation of natural resources.

Conflicts involve a variety of private and public actors, military men and civilians, not reducible to the governing groups and rebels—whence the straddling between the economic interests of firms and networks supervising revenues in an official or unofficial manner, on the one hand, and political and military forces, whether official or parallel, on the other. Oil and mining companies pursue strategies that seek to defend their revenue positions against competitors by making payments to finance the established authorities or rebels that are likely to take power. This strategy of having two irons in the fire is seen in the Elf oil company's support for Dos Santos and Savimbi in Angola and for Sassou Nguesso and Lissouba in the Congo.

Thus we have seen new conglomerate configurations appear in the Democratic Republic of the Congo that correspond to dishonest practices with regard to the old rules set up by the great oligopolies. These new conglomerates result from joint ventures between companies connected with the armies of Uganda or Zimbabwe, or with Israeli interests (Bayart et al., 1997). The economy of plunder is handled by a consortium of businessmen, mercenaries, arms merchants, and security companies confronted by the weakness of governments. We also see a whole Mafia developing around narcotics trafficking that is a source of violence.

## The tangle of factors and conflicts

Conflicts result from a tangle of factors each of which has its own temporality. They renew unresolved, age-old battles between groups (Arab-Berbers vs. Black Africans, Islam vs. animism and Christianity, nomadic shepherds vs. sedentary farmers, raiders vs. their victims, Islamicized commercial networks vs. creoles and natives) and at the same time result from economic, social, environmental, and political crises.

They take place within nations but also have a regional dimension when the actions of governments or militias affect neighboring countries. They result from identity crises against the background of the disintegration of institutions and territorial fragmentation. The preceding analysis tried to analyze and hierarchize explanatory factors but cannot include sequences and interactions leading to unregulated processes. The initial impetus may be minor, but once triggered, violent conflicts can become uncontrollable. Violence gives rise to poverty, exclusion, and an absence of institutions, all of which feed conflicts.

According to Kaplan's sociobiological thesis, the factors of *culture and civilization* allow us to rethink these new conflicts in terms of demographic pressures confronting rare factors. Wars become all the more probable when religion and politics, the absolute and the relative, the infinite and the finite are conflated. Religious fundamentalism has largely been substituted for nationalism and socialism as a societal project. However, Africa is little involved in these conflicts between civilizations, even if the internal violence in Sudan and the fighting between Eritrea and Ethiopia can be considered in part as conflicts between Christians and Muslims. On the other hand, Islamist networks more or less connected with Al Qaeda have established themselves in the Horn of Africa (Sudan, Somalia, Sahara). Black Islam has its roots in poverty, exclusion, and frustration (Ngoupandé, 2003). When there are crises, ethnic and religious references immediately become central to political rhetoric and the complexity of situations is reduced to identities or combats between the forces of evil and the forces for good. Thus in Côte d'Ivoire, as in many African societies, Pentecostal movements testifying to the confusion of the moral, the

religious, and the political confront a rise in the instrumentalization of religion by the imams in the northern part of
the country.

*Political* factors are obviously also essential, whether they
involve a lack of legitimacy on the part of the established
authorities, the disappearance of sociopolitical compromises, quarrels among leaders for access to power, the disintegration of citizenship, the desire for new territorial configurations, or exclusion from citizenship. Conflicts are all the
more likely to the extent that systems for monopolizing
wealth used by those holding power do not result in redistribution, supervision, and sanctions. War can thus have a
political goal: acceding to power through the use of force. It
takes an ethnic form insofar as ethnicity has become a
power issue. Inequality of access to positions of responsibility and competition for power and control over resources
create tensions between groups on the basis of identity (ethnic or religious). Diasporas, conglomerates, or regional powers rely on these factions. Many states no longer control
their territories or respect for law and order through a
monopoly on the legitimate use of force.

Strictly *military* factors are numerous. Armed conflicts are
connected more with inadequate government military
budgets than with excessive military budgets. Only the war
between Ethiopia and Eritrea is a conventional war between
states. Africa accounted for 10 percent of official arms
imports in 1985, but only 2 percent in 1995. As a result of
the end of the Cold War, the decrease in conflicts, and
budgetary adjustments, Africa's military spending dropped
from 20 billion dollars in 1985 to 8.1 billion dollars in 1995,
or from 3.5 percent of its total GDP to 2.8 percent. Military
spending increased from 5.5 billion constant dollars in 1995

to 7.1 billion constant dollars in 2004. Five countries account for almost three-quarters of these expenditures: South Africa (2.65 billion, or 1.6 percent of GDP), Angola (1.32 billion, or 4.7 percent of GDP), Nigeria (0.52 billion, or 1.2 percent of GDP), Ethiopia (0.34 billion, or 4.3 percent of GDP), and Eritrea (0.15 or 19.4 percent of GDP) (Source: SIPRI, 2005).

Wars are all the easier to conduct because traffic in light weapons has developed through recycling and the sale of surplus weapons from Eastern Europe. It is estimated that 100 million weapons are in circulation in Africa. Arms dealers are connected with Mafia-like networks, whether the latter are involved in narcotics, "conflict diamonds," oil, or money-laundering. The price of arms has fallen sharply. In some African countries, a Kalashnikov AK-47 costs less than ten dollars. Mercenaries, militias, and child soldiers are playing an increasing role in African wars. When conflicts end in one area, they generally move to a neighboring area (as when conflicts in Liberia and Sierra Leone moved to Côte d'Ivoire, when Rwandan Hutus moved into Congo and the Democratic Republic of the Congo, or when the Janjaweed militias moved from southern to western Sudan). Children in precarious situations find more or less forced recruitment into armed forces to be a way of surviving, and are resocialized by violence. The low opportunity cost of military activities, especially for child soldiers, results from unemployment, desocialization, and children not being in school. Regular armies and forces maintaining order have often disappeared. Then "solrebs" (soldiers during the daytime, rebels at night) appear, along with mercenaries, clan cleavages, and even private militias, reflecting the disintegration of national armies and the mobilizing of child soldiers. Here again, configurations differ depending on the country.

Private security forces, mercenaries (notably Belgian and South African), child soldiers, and violent oligopolies are playing growing roles in areas not controlled by governments (refugee camps, border zones, urban neighborhoods). Militias connected with religious or ethnic communities and traditional forces are increasingly active alongside public actors. New actors are appearing with the multiplication and the ongoing decomposition and recomposition of those involved in the violence. Conflicts are rarely confrontations between organized, opposing groups leading either to a military victory or to agreements between rebel leaders and the government. They involve civilians, itinerant fighters and soldiers available to warlords, and swaggering buffoons.

*Geopolitical* factors are important. After the end of the Cold War, the hegemonic powers largely withdrew from Africa, though a recent shift has led to interventions by Great Britain in Sierra Leone, France in Côte d'Ivoire (Operation Unicorn), and the European Union in the Democratic Republic of the Congo (Operation Artemis), and to an increased American presence (the military base in Djibouti, presence in the Sahel and Sahara). The end of the Cold War and of the bipolar world is reflected in processes of territorial fracturing and fragmentation. The peace dividends have not been invested in reducing factors leading to wars. There are new hegemonic stakes connected with oil and the battle against terrorism. Numerous African conflicts are linked to a fragmentation of the national territory not controlled by a strong government, and to transnational networks (diasporas, conglomerates, regional powers) with alliances and allegiances. In 2005, Zimbabwe was involved in a war with the Democratic Republic of the Congo in order to oppose the leadership of South Africa. Burkina Faso was present in Côte d'Ivoire in connection with Charles Taylor in Liberia. Some conflicts are about control over territory (access to the ocean for Ethiopia and Eritrea). In Chad, the Zaghawa in power in 2006 were threatened by rebels coming from Sudan, whereas events in Darfur led many people to take refuge in Chad. Like Sudan, Chad plays China and the United States off against each other for political support, while France seeks to maintain its positions in order to defend the use of the French language, maintain an equilibrium between the Arab-Muslim world and the Black Animist and Christian world, and avoid domino-effects in the region. The conflicts in Sudan, Ethiopia, Eritrea, and Angola have been largely connected with arms supplied by China, which makes use of its role on the UN Security Council and allows certain countries to evade sanctions imposed by the international community. In Somalia, a country that disintegrated into three zones after more than fifteen years of war and 400,000 dead and then was overthrown by the Ethiopian invasion, the Islamists, who are supported by Eritrea and some of whom are connected with Al Qaeda, are fighting warlords backed by the United States and Ethiopia. In June 2006 they took power in Mogadishu.

The areas of armed conflict in Africa thus result from the resurgence of models of ethnic, religious, or nationalist identity, the bankruptcy of states based on the rule of law and sovereignties that have collapsed, the interventions of regional and international powers, and a rise in the power of international criminal organizations.

*Darfur, a crime against humanity tolerated*

After twenty years' war between northern and southern Sudan that caused more than 1.5 million deaths and more than 4 million displaced persons and refugees, the fighting has now shifted to the west. The development of oil production in the south, the changed configurations after September 11, 2001, and plain fatigue have created a new situation. The conflict in Darfur—an area in western Sudan the size of France—began in February 2003, but was at that point overshadowed by the negotiations taking place in southern Sudan. To date, it has resulted in more than 200,000 deaths by violence and famine and more than 1.5 million refugees. The international community has failed to avoid a humanitarian crisis that has been called a "quasi-genocide" and a "crime against humanity" (United Nations, January 2005). The conflict is being fought between the Sudanese People's Liberation Army (SPLA) and the Justice and Equality Movement (JEM), on the one hand, and government forces and the Janjaweed militias on the other. The latter—"fiendish horsemen or bandits armed with Kalashnikovs"—are mercenaries armed by the government who pillage, burn, and rape. The pro-government militias attack chiefly civilians, especially women, whom they call "slaves or black slaves." The fracture lines are multiple and cannot be reduced to an opposition between "Africans" and "Arabs." The people are black andMuslim, and they speak Arabic.

There is a conjunction of many different factors in a context of the differentiation of rights to land and the impossibility of settling ancestral conflicts in the traditional ways. This conflict is explained historically by the central authorities' marginalization of western Sudan, by a revival of ancestral raiding, and by battles over land that emerged during the 1979-85 droughts that rendered sedentary Arab or Arabized nomadic livestock-raisers. There has been an exacerbation of the difference in "identity" between Arabs or Arabized nomadic livestock-raisers claiming to be descended from a single ancestor and to be authentic Muslims, on the one hand, and the Islamized "non-Arab Africans" who are for the most part farmers (Fur, Beri, Massalit, Zaghawa) on the other. After the cessation of the fighting between north and south, this conflict has provided an outlet for the Sudanese armed forces and militias. The war is also about economic development—gaining control over oil and over land for agro-industrial groups on the Persian Gulf.

During 2006 and 2007 the conflict in Sudan and Darfur spread to Chad and the Central African Republic along with refugee groups and trans-border rebels. Darfur is a sanctuary for rebels from neighboring Chad. The refugee camps in Chad are breeding grounds for Sudanese rebels, and the Zaghawa ethnic group lives on both sides of the border. Thus we now find in Chad the same fracture line between white and black Africa, ethnic or clan differences, and religious, linguistic, and climatic differences. Access to power is achieved by force of arms. The borders are very long. The population is one of the poorest in the world, despite or because of oil. The people have a warrior tradition. Oil has accentuated the conflicts. In 2006, the Chad opposition took advantage of the Sudanese sanctuary, whereas refugees from Darfur were in Chad. France had a military presence and a cooperative agreement with Chad, but not a defense agreement.

The international community has shown itself to be par-

ticularly powerless. Sudan has received the support of the
Arab League, of Libya, and of Russia. China uses its veto on
the UN Security Council to advance its oil and strategic
interests in Sudan. Humanitarian action is very difficult.
The African Union has sent 7,000 troops (The African
Union Mission in Sudan), but they are ill equipped and lack
a clear mandate. In its resolutions 1590, 1591, and 1593
(March 2005), the United Nations planned to send 10,000
men and establish an arms embargo. In its Resolution 1564
(September 18, 2004), the Security Council had recommended oil sanctions against Sudan. In early 2007, the
Sudanese government opposed this interventionist force.
The result was an agreement on a mixed force composed of
both African Union and United Nations troops and the creation of a corridor from Chad permitting the delivery of
humanitarian aid (June 2007).

*Somalia*

For the past two decades, Somalia has been experiencing a
clan-based Balkanization and chaos that has resulted in
300,000 to 500,000 deaths. Each of the clans has its own
militia. The Somalis speak the same language (Somali), they
are Sunni Muslims, and they constitute a single people with
a pastoral tradition. The conflicts are between clans. From
1992 to 1994, interventions by international forces and the
United States experienced a defeat recounted in the film
*Black Hawk Down.* The Islamic courts, supported in particular by Eritrea, took power in the summer of 2006 against the
heads of factions. They represent various tendencies, even
radical Islamism, and have been accused of being an African
version of the Afghan Taliban. In late 2006, the transitional

government supported militarily by Ethiopia and the United States, and indirectly by Kenya, Uganda, and Yemen, retook control of Mogadishu, though they did not control the warlords. There is a risk of guerrilla conflicts between militias, factions, and warlords, or even of the whole region going to war in the context of the opposition between *jihad* and the battle against terrorism.

## The prevention and resolution of African conflicts

The means for preventing conflicts and maintaining peace are multiple and involve several international, regional, and national actors. *Diplomatic* means range from negotiation (mediation) to sanctions (embargoes, sanctions of officials). Diplomacy, which takes time, skill, and credibility, does not eliminate the deep causes of conflicts, but it can prevent the latter and attenuate their consequences. There are also *military* means, ranging from the simple presence of armed forces to local or regional interventions; *political* means, involving respect for signed agreements and the implementation of reforms affecting the roots of these conflicts; *financial* means, involving compensation for the losses of those who lay down their weapons and have to find jobs; *humanitarian* means, involving aid in emergencies; and *juridical* means, even if humanitarian laws of war and the numerous international conventions are relatively helpless when faced by these new, multiform conflicts and guerrilla actions. These means are viable only if the structural causes and deep factors constituted by poverty, exclusion, regional inequalities, a lack of respect for democratic rules, the non-transparency of economic and political circuits, and participation in a worldwide criminal economy are eliminated.

Reconciliation has emerged as the way to move beyond situations of extreme violence.[6] When confronted by collapsing states, the role of a third-party mediator guaranteeing respect for the social contract also has to be performed by international and regional organizations, or even by foreign powers. But this can be justified only if liberal globalization and global economic disorder is regulated at the same time and if the circuits of international Mafias, offshore financial institutions, arms dealers, and connections between corrupters and corrupt are controlled by northern hemisphere powers (cf. the Kimberly accord to establish traceability for conflict diamonds).

The UN is present in Africa (more than 45,000 soldiers costing 2.5 billion dollars in 2004, not counting civilians). Many different African actors and organizations are engaged in preventing and managing conflicts in Africa. The African Union, unlike the Organization of African Unity (which respects states' sovereignty), is increasingly intervening in Burundi and Darfur. The West African Economic Community, with its group for monitoring and implementing the cease-fire (ECOMOG), has obtained significant results in Liberia. Nonetheless, it has been less present in West African conflicts, which sometimes oppose its members. The South African Development Community (SADC) intervened in the Democratic Republic of the Congo, and South Africa, which has been a member of this organization since 1994, plays an increasingly high-profile diplomatic role.

Western military power is more involved in Africa. France, whose military presence fell from 8,000 troops in 1985 to 6,000 in 2001, has played an increasingly important role in Côte d'Ivoire, in Ituri (a province of the Democratic Republic of the Congo), and in the Reinforcement of African Peacekeeping Capacities (RECAMP) program, which is becoming Europeanized. The United Kingdom, which has a fund for the prevention of conflicts, is seeking to contain conflicts in and around Sierra Leone, the Great Lakes region, Sudan, and Angola, and has pursued a very coherent strategy (massive aid, personalized dialogue). The British Military Advisory and Training Team (BMATT) is the British equivalent of the French RECAMP. Moreover, the United Kingdom has supported ECOMOG in Liberia and Sierra Leone. As for the United States, since September 11, 2001, they have set up the Pan-Sahel Initiative, and the Pentagon provides African governments with advice, training, and information. In addition, the United States has military bases in Djibouti and Diego Garcia. It seeks to strengthen regional and sub-regional integration and to develop states' internal capacities. This is the first intervention carried out by the United States independent of NATO. The UN is present notably through the United Nations Mission in the Democratic Republic of the Congo (MONUC).

Post-conflict priorities are the disarmament, demobilization, and re-entry into civilian life of members of the armed forces and militias, the reconstruction of a civilian bureaucracy, and the emergency rehabilitation and reestablishment of the rule of law. These actions can be carried out by military men in association with humanitarian organizations. But they seek to deal first of all with the deep causes of conflicts, particularly control over natural resources and the Extractive Industries Transparency Initiative (EITI) supported by the Commission for Africa (2005).

## Problems of Sustainable Development

Sustainable development is "a development that allows present needs to be met without compromising the ability of future generations to meet their own needs" (Brundtland Report, 1987), or "development that gives future generations as many or more opportunities than we have." It has economic, social, environmental, and demographic dimensions. It presupposes arbitrations between short-term priorities for survival and the long-term preservation of the biosphere.

### Demographic and political issues

*Only men have wealth and power.*      —Montchrestien, 1615

Africa is fundamentally a continent that is being populated and changing the way it occupies its territory. From a historical point of view, it is catching up demographically and returning to the place in world population that it had before the slave trade (12 percent).

*Demographic challenges*

Africa, after having stagnated demographically until World War II, is the continent on which demographic growth is highest. The population has quadrupled since 1950, rising from 175 million to more than 700 million. It is supposed to reach 1.2 billion in 2030. However, it remains poorly populated. The distribution of the population is very uneven. The average population density is thirty individuals per square kilometer, but the density is ten to a hundred times higher in areas with arable land. We can speak of an "empty triangle" (Dubresson, Raison, 2003) that is under-populated, under-administered, and isolated. The occupation of the territory is correlated not with physical constraints (climate, vegetation, soil quality, etc.) but with protection against disease and war. The slave trade has certainly played a role, but the coastal regions that were most affected are also the most densely populated (e.g., Nigeria).

The familial system is characterized by great fecundity; children are often entrusted to family members who raise them, but there is also a high percentage of orphans (12 percent, of whom one-third have lost their parents to AIDS). The family unit plays a central role in reproduction and in care for pre- and post-productive individuals in the absence of a retirement system and official welfare provisions. In most African countries, a decline of the synthetic index of fecundity (5.5 in 2005) appeared only ten years ago, in a period of economic crisis. Nonetheless, we note that contraceptive measures are little used, and religious authorities generally encourage large families. There is a debate about whether there is individualization or solidarity in a period of difficulties, a solidarity of crisis or a crisis of solidarity.

Maternal mortality and infantile and youth mortality, which had sharply declined since World War II, has been increasing for the past ten years, chiefly because of wars (the Rwandan genocide and the AIDS epidemic). Crisis mortality has caused life expectancy to fall by fifteen years in Southern Africa.

The effects of demography on the economy, the social system, and the environment come into play only when mediated by institutions and the strategies of actors. There are Malthusian situations in which demographic pressure creates great tensions (Burundi, Rwanda), but there are also situations in which creative pressures are connected with high population densities (the Kenyan high plateaus or the Bamileke in Cameroon). Past developments show that African subsistence agriculture has, on the whole, met the demographic challenge. Commercialized agriculture practiced by the peasants has increased in tandem with the ratio of the non-agricultural to the agricultural population. Commercialized subsistence agriculture has gradually connected with the market and has provided a growing share of the mercantile GDP, and also of the agricultural GDP at the expense of agricultural exports and subsistence crops consumed by the producers. On the whole, the development of population density in rural areas has followed the development of urban markets.

This demographic explosion has led to both creative and destructive pressures (notably on ecosystems), but it also has high costs given the pace of the necessary demographic investments and a demographic pyramid with a very broad base. Education for all by 2015 would suppose that school enrollments would rise from 65 million to 140 million. More than half the population is less than fifteen years old. Institutions that are integrating, such as the family, schools and places of employment, are put in question and the future often seems to be blocked. The young are very quickly changing their political models. Mugabe and Gbagbo have become heroes supplanting Mandela, Nyerere, and Nkrumah, the leaders of the period of independence who are largely unknown to young people today. Young people aspire to training, employment, and imported models of consumption.

## Migration and urbanization

The mobility of the population is a constant in African history. It is connected in particular with resilience when faced with instabilities and shocks coming from the outside. It is at the heart of adaptation to changes. The main contemporary migrations are from the Sahelian regions to coastal areas and from the countries of Southern Africa to South Africa. They assume that land is available and accessible and that rights will be given to migrants. Mobility is also forced, with many displaced persons and refugees (more than 16 million).

Migration is part of the process of rapid urbanization. Between 1930 and 2030, urban areas will have absorbed 70 percent of population growth. Demographic concentration has to be accompanied by suitable infrastructural facilities (water, sanitation, transportation, etc.) that are adapted to the needs and a financing that allows the city to be a motor for development and not the vector for new forms of poverty leading to delinquency, insecurity, and pollution. The major dynamic processes will proceed from the urban popular economy.

The city has become the symbolic site of modernity. African cities are less and less connected with the state. In the cities, there is a break with coercive values (forced marriage, clitoridectomy, polygamy), but there is also a risk of disintegration. Urbanization plays an ambivalent role in terms of imitation of foreign models, but it also plays a role in creating markets that make it possible to promote agricultural products, especially those from the areas around the cities (market gardens). In general, we see a shift of the value added in rural areas toward urban areas within agro-alimentary chains (transformation, storage, distribution, preparation of meals, etc.). Most of the informal urban economy concerns this domain. However, we must also distinguish between cities that are dependent on revenue and/or extraverted, and cities that have a stimulating effect on agricultural and agro-industrial dynamics. The image of the creativity and ingeniousness of urban popular economies is opposed to that of the disintegration of the social bond, of violence, deviancy, and even delinquency. With the decline in employment, the working class often becomes an underclass, and "peasants without food or shelter become lawless vagabonds" (Marx, *Capital*, 1865). Great cities such as Lagos (12 million inhabitants), Johannesburg (8 million), Kinshasa (6 million), and Nairobi (4 million) are out of control, with environmental, social, and security problems.

Sometimes a dualistic distinction is drawn between cities and countryside, between urban centers as a universe of order and the areas around them as places of exclusion, poverty, and even criminality and deviancy. In reality, there are only permeable borders, hybridizations, social innovations. The borders between cities and rural areas are transgressed by networks that face in both directions. What is peripheral from one point of view becomes central or normative from another.

*Migratory pressures and international migrations*

Most African migrations, whether forced or voluntary (currently involving 16 million people) are internal to the African continent. They are largely substitutes for migrations toward other continents. The latter are less connected with demographic pressures or with poverty than with the existence of migratory networks set up in the past. Thus Senegal's Middle Valley was a departure point for Europe. However, we seed major changes resulting from the limits of regional African migration, on the one hand, and new points of departure (for example, the Great Lakes) on the other. The main emigrations in West Africa are from Cape Verde, Senegal, Mali, and Burkina Faso to Côte d'Ivoire, Ghana, Gabon, and Europe. In East Africa, main emigrations are from Ethiopia and Sudan to Europe, the Persian Gulf States, and in central and Southern Africa, the main emigrations are from the Democratic Republic of the Congo, Malawi, Botswana, and Mozambique toward South Africa. In France, 18 percent of immigrants come from sub-Saharan Africa. Immigration from the Sahel is rural in origin; that from coastal and central Africa is more urban, more skilled, and less redistributive. Migratory networks lead to major transfers in the areas of departure and to a self-renewing source of new migrants. The funds returned by migrants are estimated at twice the amounts of aid. Nonetheless, in zones of chaos (e.g., the Great Lakes) we see forced migrations only marginally connected with networks. Emigration increasingly involves educated groups. Africans represent 7 percent of the migration of skilled workers within the countries of the Organization for Economic Cooperation and Development (OECD). The income of the 200,000 Africans living the United States is estimated at 750 billion dollars, more than twice the GDP of sub-Saharan Africa.

The demographic imbalances between Africa and Europe (whether in terms of the rate of growth or of structure by age that are connected with growing gaps in income can only lead to heavy pressure to migrate to industrial countries perceived as Eldorados. Migration to Europe has changed with programs to allow immigrants' families to join them and with clandestine immigration. Regulation through policies of cooperation or co-development is a major strategic issue.

## Issues in economic and social development

Economic development differs from growth measured in terms of the amount of value added. It implies both increases in productivity that are equitably distributed and forces that allow this process to be endogenized. It also implies that there are several developments that are moving away from imitation of the West.

In 2005, eight "Millennium Development Objectives" were set by the UN, to be achieved by 2015: reducing extreme poverty and hunger, providing primary education for all, promoting equality of the sexes, reducing infant mortality, improving maternal health, fighting AIDS, malaria, and other diseases, guaranteeing a sustainable environment, and establishing a partnership for development. Economic performance is very inadequate in relation to these objectives. Several aid and debt reduction measures have tried to bring observed results closer to the objectives.

The usual image of African poverty is paradoxical. On the one hand, poverty affects the whole continent. But on the other, Africa has redistributive mechanisms that work, even if some of them are excluded from community networks and state redistributions. Poverty, which is multidimensional and irreducible to revenue, can be analyzed as a diminution of rights connected with exclusion from the market, public goods, and social ties (Sen, 1981). Vulnerability to shocks and the precariousness associated with risks are more important than poverty itself. The urban model is running out of steam because of the hopes of benefits it arouses and the modes of urban management to which it leads. The educative model is in crisis because people who earn diplomas no longer can hope to get salaried positions. In the short term, the informal economy is dealing with this crisis (Michailhof, 1993). Economic liberalization is leading to a growing gap between the aspirations of a consumption model and what most people can actually consume.

The crucial role of training and education in the process of development is the object of a consensus that seems to be even stronger in the new economy of information, knowledge, and cognitive capitalism. In few domains are the issues as conflictual, whether in terms of values and knowledge transmitted, tensions between universalism and particularism, or differing access to schooling depending on social category or gender. More than 40 million children are not in school, with a significant gap between boys and girls (9 percent more boys than girls are in school). Education for all seems to be a mirage that keeps receding as one moves toward it.

Public health issues are essential. Africa does not have a public and private health system allowing it to prevent diseases and to care for the ill. Health is a strategic issue that concerns national public actors, the medical profession, NGOs, pharmaceutical firms, and international aid programs. The centralized public health system is giving way to elementary healthcare and contributions by families that are not able to deal with the situation. The AIDS virus has become the second most frequent cause of death after malaria, and causes ten times as many deaths as wars. There are more than 25 million HIV-positive individuals in Africa. Southern Africa is particularly affected. AIDS has economic consequences (decapitalizing elites and leading to unbearable expenses), demographic consequences (decline in life expectancy and stagnation in the most affected countries), and social consequences (beginning with 4 million orphans) (Fassin, 2005).

## Environmental issues

Environmental issues have become increasingly acute with desertification, the reduction in biodiversity, urban pollution, and deterioration of the soil. In the context of poverty, vulnerable actors have little resilience to confront natural catastrophes. Priority is given to survival and short-term problems at the expense of management of patrimonies in an intergenerational perspective. Earlier regulations of ecosystems are put in question by the rapidity of change. The biotope depends on delicate balances (a water source, a few trees in the Sahel). Within ecosystems, deforestation, climatic changes, energy needs, access to water, and a decline in biodiversity are all interconnected. The management of environmental risks, which has traditionally been part of patrimonial strategies, has been challenged by demographic pressures, technological developments, changes in institutional rules, the development of commercial values, and technocratic politics. In many cases the headlong rush to control non-renewable resources (mines, fishing grounds) is leading to a "tragedy of free goods" (called "common goods" by Hardin).

## Climatic issues

In 2005, drought and desertification threatened 250 million Africans. But because proactive strategies have not been adopted, this figure is likely to increase over the next twenty years (Bied-Charreton). Africa is undergoing climatic change and its effects in terms of drought (in both northern and southern areas) and flooding (equatorial Africa). At the same time, Africa contributes 7 percent of the emissions of greenhouse gases (produced mainly by the burning of forests) without benefiting from the developmental mechanisms peculiar to the Kyoto Protocol, such as free navigation. Biodiversity (the diversity of wild species, fauna and flora, intra-species diversities, and conservation over time) is an element in ecosystems' resilience in responding to climatic changes. The forest is a well of carbon.

## Energy issues

Ninety percent of Africa's energy consumption is connected with forest products in arid zones. Wood-based energy is only partially renewable, since its increasing use aggravates local deforestation and the deterioration of the soil, especially in the Sahel or in Madagascar. Electrification covers chiefly the centers of capital cities and presupposes heavy investment. Africa has considerable hydroelectric potential. These resources are located mainly in the humid part of Africa in the center of the continent (the Congo River with the dam at Inga, the Zambezi River, the Nile) and they are often far distant from the places where they are consumed (the urbanized zones and the dry part of Africa).

*The geopolitics of water*

The most worrying threat is the foreseeable water shortages in many areas. One African out of two lacks access to
potable water. Need it be said that one American consumes
on average 700 liters of water a day, compared with 300
liters for a European and 30 liters for an African? Africa consumes 4.7 percent of the world's water and fourteen countries have water shortages, even though the continent has
seventeen major rivers and 160 lakes. Providing potable
water is one of the priorities of the Millennium Development Objectives initiative, and it was central to the discussions at the Earth Summit held in Johannesburg in 2002,
which sought to reduce by half the number of people without potable water before 2015.

With rare exceptions, African societies are not hydraulic
civilizations. Only 4 percent of cultivated land is irrigated:
South Africa, the Office du Niger in Mali[7], Senegal's Middle
Valley, and the Gezireh dams in Sudan. On the other hand,
rivers and lakes play a central role in delimiting borders and
naming states (Pourtier). Water is very unevenly distributed
and leads us to contrast one Africa that lacks water with
another that has an excess of water (floods). Many countries
such as Botswana, Gambia, Mauritania, Niger, and Sudan
depend on other countries for water.

Water supplies concern first of all consumer sectors (agriculture consumes 70 percent, industry 20 percent). Water is
also a major risk factor as a source of diseases (onchocerco-
sis, trypanosomiasias, parasitic diseases, malaria). Water is
both a good with a certain cost and a right. It also has symbolic meaning.

Water is a geopolitical resource and when proactive
strategies are lacking, it may be one of the essential factors

in twenty-first century conflicts, as it is or has been in Egypt and Sudan, in Ethiopia and Somalia, in South Africa and Lesotho, or the countries along the Nile or the Niger rivers (Bouguerra, 2004). It was already central to the Berlin Conference discussions regarding the free circulation of the Congo and Niger rivers. We see water becoming rarer, a tendency toward decreasing rainfall, and lakes drying up (Lake Chad). Agriculture, which is characterized by poor control over water, has increasing needs. The farmers of the Sahel are infringing on pasture zones and water sources. Regional cooperation is thus crucial for preventing conflicts (cf. the projects in the Nile basin and the forest basin in Congo, the Sourou Valley Development Authority (AMVS), the development of the Senegal River, the Niger basin, and the transborder basins of the South African Development Community (SADC).

*Deforestation*

Rapid deforestation modifies microclimates, exposes land to erosion, and reduces biodiversity. Slash-and-burn cultivation and energy needs are the two factors chiefly responsible. In addition, there is over-exploitation of forest areas in order to export wood. However, we must distinguish between deforestation in West Africa and Madagascar, which is very rapid, and that in central Africa, which is advancing less quickly. The risks of deterioration in the cultivated areas of sub-humid parts of sub-Saharan Africa result from excessive pressure on soils that diminishes their fertility. The deterioration of the soil produced by shortening fallow periods and over-pasturing was pointed out long ago (Harroy, *Afrique, terre qui meurt*, 1941).

*Issues relating to biodiversity and biotechnologies*

Several kinds of knowledge about the biotope and about the immediate environment and a cultural heritage connected with a natural heritage make it possible to manage complexity. However, there is a risk that this know-how and biodiversity will be destroyed, that plants will be patented, and that technological uniformity will be imposed in the name of efficiency, profitability, and power relationships. For centuries, indeed for millennia, there has been free access to phylogenetic resources. The selection of varieties is carried out by farming that leads to genetic intermingling. These rights held by peasants and seed producers now are now in opposition to oligopolies that have property rights to genes. Today, whole areas of knowledge, notably those connected with genetic resources or food products, have been appropriated by private groups in accord with the only creditworthy market. The result is that research is oriented by the priorities of Northern Hemisphere countries and questions concerning temperate counties (where 92.6 percent of the population of rich countries lives). With biotechnologies—a set of technologies seeking to exploit industrially micro-organisms, animal and vegetable cells, and their constituents—genetic resources have become a major new source of wealth.

Genetically-modified organisms (GMOs) reveal major problems relating to alimentary options (technological and scientific innovations vs. ecological prudence, goods held in common vs. the patentability and appropriation of the living, northern hemisphere agro-industries vs. southern hemisphere peasant agriculture). There is a debate as to GMOs' effects. On the one hand, they are supposed to produce larger harvests, resistance to stress, and lower pesticide costs. On the other, a probable decrease in biodiversity, health or environmental risks (genetic pollution), and peasants' dependence on seed producers is predicted. The United States Agency for International Development (USAID) has become a vector for Monsanto for spreading GMOs by promoting contagious effects (from Burkina Faso to Mali, for example).

In Africa, there are normative conflicts between the Organization of African Unity's model law on access to biological resources and the 1977 Bangui Accord, which came into force on 28 February 2002 and includes WTO constraints. The OAU model law recognizes the inalienable and collective rights of communities and farmers' rights, to which the rights of seed selectors are subordinated.

## Problems of Food Supply

The geopolitics of human catastrophes can be illustrated by famines. Famines result from shocks to food supply systems and vulnerable populations that decision-makers have been unable to anticipate or limit, and that lead to effects of contagion and large numbers of deaths. They reflect a lack of resilience on the part of vulnerable actors confronting catastrophes.

### Famines and alimentary insecurities

Famines are numerous in Africa, even if today there are surplus food supplies on the global level (Von Braun et al., 1996). In Africa, there were famines before colonization (in the Empires of Ghana, Mali, and Songhaï) and during colo-

nization (Ethiopia, 1888-1892). Recent famines have occurred in Ethiopia (1972-74, 1984-85), Sudan, Lesotho
(1983-85), Mozambique, Nigeria, Niger, Angola, Zaïre,
Uganda, Somalia, Liberia, Zimbabwe and Southern Africa
(2005-2006), the Sahel, notably in Niger, and the Horn of
Africa (2005-2006). Two hundred million Africans are mal-
nourished.

## Factors explaining alimentary insecurity and famine

There is a whole list of explanatory factors: lack of water,
poor management, demographic pressure, the effects of
conflicts and the AIDS virus, and the instrumentalization of
food aid. Half the food crises involve civil wars, displaced
persons, and refugees.

Four main explanations can be distinguished:

*Lack of availability*

Long term, the factors determining access to food supplies are 1) productivity per hectare, which is low or stag-
nant; 2) the limited surface cultivated in relation to the size
of the population; rural populations continuing to grow,
despite urbanization; 3) decreasing consumption and purchasing power; 4) shocks that have to do with the vagaries
of climate, social problems, epidemics, and speculation.

African agriculture has made little progress, though there
is commercial subsistence agriculture for the villages. Modes
of cultivation range from slash and burn to irrigated cultivation, via modes of cultivation that make heavy use of
labor, mechanization, and basic materials like seeds. Agri-

culture in industrialized countries is about one hundred times more productive than African agriculture. From 1970 to 1995, rainfall decreased by 30 to 50 percent in the Sahel, with negative effects on agriculture and livestock-raising as well as on health. The African Monsoon Multidisciplinary Analyses (AMMA) program seeks to predict the monsoon, which provides the only rainfall in the Sahel, where water is the main factor limiting food production.

*Breakdowns in the market*

While African markets function competitively, equilibrium prices make it possible to avoid shortages. The more the market grows, the more transportation costs decrease, the more the speed of the circulation of food supplies increases, and the more the risks of famine decrease. In reality, several elements can explain why markets do not play the efficient role they are expected to play. In a situation of imperfect information a strategy involving multiple activities or extensive cultivation is generally preferable, given option values (connected with the reversibility of the decision). The liberal argument according to which speculators play a stabilizing role presupposes that no errors of prediction are made and that the speculators called hoarders compete with each other. However, these speculators are usually in cahoots with the government and have a buyers' monopoly. To these theoretical arguments concerning markets' informational and allocative deficiencies, we can add infrastructural and logistical defects and a lack of market integration.

*Lack of rights*

As Sen (1981) showed, access to food is a function of allocations and entitlements. Famine also depends on a lack of "capability," which is a function of the individual (aptitudes, needs) and of a social organization that allows being and doing. Societies have established rules permitting pre-, post-, and non-productive individuals to survive (Meillassoux, 1975), prohibiting the convertibility of subsistence goods and prestige goods or of money derived from subsistence agriculture and revenue agriculture (e.g., rice and coffee in Madagascar). But these rules are broken or disturbed in crisis situations. Empirical studies of the Wollo (1973) and the Sahel 1973-74) have shown that even when food supplies were sufficient some social groups went hungry because of a sharp rise in prices or because they had lost rights.

*The geopolitics of famine*

Malnutrition is naturally connected with poverty, low agricultural productivity, and breakdowns in markets, but conflicts and plundering are the determining factors. Conflicts mobilize the work force, lead to areas of insecurity, and are characterized by levies of produce and receipts. They prevent people from attenuating risks by managing reserves, moving, or engaging in multiple activities. Very often, they are ways of wiping out a dominated group by means of hunger. Food blockades have always been used as a weapon against enemies and minorities. Democracies have experienced shortages but never famines. Humanitarian aid can also play a perverse role. It is often used to keep the war going or is monopolized by governments at the expense of the population (as in Somalia). It is difficult and dangerous to get humanitarian aid into many countries at war (cf. the warlords and pirates in Somalia who seize aid and attack NGOs). It results from disinformation on the part of authorities seeking to capture the maximum of aid or aid agencies that exaggerate the needs in order to compensate for donor fatigue. It is also a way of draining off the surpluses in industrialized countries, a factor of competition among local producers, and a stake in the appropriation of revenues by the political powers. It is also important to take into account the strategies adopted by the great international powers. The United States has played a role in Ethiopian famines by using food supplies as way to bring down the Marxist government. Most African countries have become dependent on food supplies that may also be used as weapons, notably supplies provided by the United States (78 percent of the corn exports), but also by France, Canada, Australia, and Argentina (these five countries account for 90 percent of world wheat exports) (Brunel, 2004).

## What are the political implications?

Public authorities and non-governmental organizations have an essential preventative role in avoiding systemic risks by using systems of rapid information and intervention. Mechanisms for setting up safety nets are necessary with regard to the most vulnerable groups excluded from the market. Stabilizing policies are no longer able to ensure a secure food supply. When famine threatens, emergency measures are imperative: help, work programs, regulating reserves. Emergency humanitarian actions become necessary but they can also ultimately make situations worse. Humanitarian catastrophes have helped change collective modes of action. Emergency aid is being substituted for development aid. Humanitarian action has become a partnership that allows crises to be managed. Many NGOs are present in this aid market, good ones alongside bad ones (Brunel, 2004). In the long run, the eradication of famines involves development policies that improve availability and accessibility by means of productivity, redistributive policies, increased access to credit for agents, support for popular initiatives, and demographic regulation.

# CHAPTER IV

# Africa and International Society

Works on international relations commonly distinguish *internal orders* through which the powers of the state having a monopoly on the legitimate use of force in a territory are expressed, on the one hand, and an *international order* in which asymmetrical powers operating in different power relationships are deployed. For several reasons, Africa largely escapes this distinction. The internal order is provided chiefly by external powers and, inversely, internal disorder has, to a lesser degree, a retroactive effect on international relations. Africa is perceived as having a capacity for producing *harm* (conflicts, migratory pressures, epidemics) more than *power*. The disintegration of colonial empires, which caused African states to emerge as actors in international society, retained a role for the former colonial powers (France, the United Kingdom), while at the same time leading to a transfer of authority to international organizations, the European Union, and the American superpower. The new international configuration is partly deterritorialized and mobilizes a variety of public and private actors that have both structural and relational powers. Africa is situated in both a territorial logic and a reticular logic.

# Africa and International Organizations

There is no international democracy in which decisions are made in accordance with the rule of one citizen, one vote, but rather systems in which the rule is one state, one vote (UN, WTO) or even one dollar, one vote (IMF, World Bank), with the great powers having the right to veto decisions. In practice, through alliances, tricks, or denial of failures, coalitions make African states actors in international society. There are conventions and international regimes, a set of principles, rules, norms, and procedures that reduce hegemony.

## The United Nations and Africa

International economic and financial institutions were created after World War II in the framework of inter-governmental relationships, separating politics from economics and based on the principle of equal sovereignty and the reality of a bipolar world dominated by the hegemonic power of the United States. The United Nations, the supreme organ of international law and negotiations among states, is also an arena in which states confront each other in function of their power, the main issue being the Security Council. Today, international relations reflect a "spatial incongruity" (Palan, 1998) between an economy that is being globalized and an international political system based on the nation-state, national sovereignty, territorialized law, and international institutions that lack supranational power even if organizations of international solidarity aspire to create a public sphere aimed at an international citizenship. The international space is structured politically by power relationships among hegemonic states with military, technological forces, and economically by oligopolistic firms and institutional stockholders. In the absence of a world government capable of imposing discipline and sanctions, a global "governmentality" is being set up through negotiations of international rules, the elaboration of norms and values, and a set of regulations guaranteed by the various actors. Thus, within international organizations, relationships of influence, negotiation, and even the imposition of decisions play a role.

## Africa and the United Nations

African countries are members of the main international organizations but they have little say in this international order. They also belong to the non-aligned movement. They all signed the nuclear non-proliferation treaty and are members of the International Atomic Energy Agency. South Africa has renounced nuclear weapons. Two African states, South Africa and Ethiopia, were among the fifty-one countries that founded the United Nations in 1945. The UN, which in 2005 had 191 member states, is playing a growing role in aid to Africa and as a force of intervention. It is situated in a multilateral framework and serves as a compass for the international community. Three African countries alternate as non-permanent members of the Security Council, and may eventually be granted one or two permanent seats on the Council. Africa participates in specialized, non-financial UN institutions: the FAO (agriculture), WHO (health), UNIDO (industrialization), UNDP (development), UNESCO (education and culture), ILO (labor), UNICEF (aid to children), and UNFPA (population). It makes its voice heard through UNCTAD, which advocates for poor countries seeking to correct the perverse effects of liberalization by connecting international trade with development.

## Africa and the Bretton Woods Institutions

Almost all African countries are members of the Bretton Woods Institutions and have recourse to the financing they provide, which leads them to be put under supervision to a certain extent.

*The International Monetary Fund (IMF)*

The IMF's mission is to "facilitate the expansion and harmonious growth of international trade and to contribute to the maintenance and development of a high level of employment and real income" (article 1). It is a fund for mutual assistance among states. It serves to provide a) multilateral and bilateral monitoring of macroeconomic monetary and exchange policies; b) programs of technical assistance.

The IMF has played a central role in normalizing African societies starting with the debt crisis of the 1980s and has led to conditional aid with the establishment of programs of stabilization and adjustment seeking to reduce financial imbalances. Signing a "standby accord" has become the condition for renegotiating debt. African ministers of finance have operated under supervision, and financial power has shifted away from parliaments to the Bretton Woods Institutions. Since 2000, facilities for strengthened structural adjustment have been transformed into facilities for reducing poverty and increasing growth in countries with low revenues. Loans are accorded to countries that set up strategic frameworks for combating poverty.

## The World Bank

The World Bank is the second pillar of the international financial institutions. The Bank's interventions in Africa have evolved over time. In the 1950s and 1960s, a culture of engineers and financing for infrastructures was dominant. In the 1970s, notably at the urging of Robert MacNamara (then president of the World Bank), financing for projects in productive sectors and support for public entities dominated. The period from the 1980s to the mid-1990s was marked by debt, macroeconomic adjustments, and a priority given to macroeconomists. Since that time, the World Bank has considerably expanded its areas of intervention (the fight against AIDS, new technologies, etc.) and has emphasized the battle against poverty, the need to strengthen institutions, and software (knowledge) as opposed to hardware (physical investments). Like the IMF, it has responded to criticism by aiming at more transparency and setting up systems for evaluation that have improved its portfolio of projects. The Heavily Indebted Poor Countries (HIPC) program has challenged the rule of not rescheduling multilateral debts and has given priority to the fight against poverty.

## Normalization and dissimulation

In addition to a rational economic discourse and successes in financial rebalancing, there is the catechism of the Washington Consensus, which mixes theoretical arguments, case studies, and success stories recommending "good policies" in terms of openness, liberalization, privatization, and "good governance" (Hibou). Adjustment refers to a sequence involving international negotiations, setting conditions, access to outside financing, reforms in political economy, and monitoring of criteria of performance showing whether countries are on track or not.

Internally, measures recommended—no matter how judicious they might be—are perceived as imposed from outside. Internal structural and institutional factors, as well as the international environment, over-determine the success of economic policies in the poorest countries. Adjustment has often modified fragile sociopolitical balances. There are conflicts regarding procedure, status, and legitimacy among programs of adjustment that depend on technical ministers and laws, for example, development plans having to do with national sovereignty and that participate in the gradual erosion of that sovereignty.

On the international level, we can speak of "the continual denial of failure" (Ferguson, 1990). Money lenders set numerous conditions that allow them to keep borrowers on a short leash. Governments take into account the risks of breaking with the international financial community, but they also expect that sanctions will not be applied or that other lenders may be found. The result is a double discourse or double governmental practices, delays in implementing measures, open conflicts and hidden resistance. Many countries no longer have reliable systems of information and have weak analytical capacities, especially in the area of macroeconomics, which prevent them from proposing alternative models or gauging the validity of the measures. Performance criteria, like the Potemkin villages that Catherine the Great visited, are sometimes deceptive façades concealing reality. The consequence is a play of simulacra.

Thus we can see the IMF and the World Bank as Janus-figures. On the one hand they play a hegemonic stabilizing role. They are largely connected with the American treasury (Stiglitz, 2003). They have set linguistic norms and won, for the time being, liberalism's ideological battle. Their technocratic discourse based on economic rationality and the power of models has led to the belief that there is only one good economic policy applied by good pupils serving as examples. Forbidden by statute to engage in politics, they are at the heart of these issues while negotiating only with governments, ensuring their internal legitimacy and external credibility with regard to the international financial community and setting conditions. But at the same time they are overwhelmed by the influence of private capital (including its most illicit forms), the play of governments (including the most prebendiary or Mafia-like of them), and the priority of security.

## The WTO and Africa

### The WTO

The General Agreement on Tariffs and Trade (GATT) signed in 1948 favored commercial multilateralism by reducing tariffs and other barriers to international trade. It was based on certain principles: the rule of non-discrimination (the most-favored-nation clause), the attempt to reduce customs duties, and the prohibition on quantitative restrictions. The principle of equality of treatment nonetheless included exceptions for customs unions and free-trade zones and acceptance of non-reciprocity and differing treatment for developing countries. It recognized that openness to the outside is a major factor in growth.

When the GATT was transformed into the World Trade Organization (WTO), trade negotiation became permanent. The WTO, which seeks to liberalize world trade, set rules, and arbitrate conflicts, is a negotiating authority in which 149 countries have a voice, but in which the great powers, which represent two thirds of world trade, impose their interests, although counter-powers are appearing among emergent countries (G20, the Group of Twenty) and even the poor countries (G90, the Group of Ninety). The WTO has included agricultural products and service industries in liberalization while at the same time accepting what the French call *l'exception culturelle*. It passed first from a system of reciprocal concessions (enlightened mercantilism) to negotiations and bargaining by products, and then to general discussions regarding all products. Concessions are perceived as costs that require compensation, whereas the standard theory of international trade shows that liberalization does not need reciprocity to improve welfare, and that within countries, in a positive-sum game, the winners can always compensate the losers. The stakes have become normative with agricultural products, services, and intellectual property rights (the WTO's Legal Aspects of Intellectual Property Relating to Trade program). They are at the heart of national sovereignty (precaution, social norms, sovereignty with respect to food supply, environmental norms). The great blocs oppose each other within the WTO, particularly with regard to agriculture: the United States, the European Union, and the Group of Twenty, the latter representing emerging countries that are more or less favorable to liberalization, with various alliances. The African countries have few trumps to play in the arena of trade negotiations. They are suffering from the perverse effects of production and export subsidies and from American and European protectionism, and they will be losers in the process of liberalization because of the erosion of preferential treatment (sugar, bananas) and ferocious competition among producers (agriculture, livestock raising, textiles).

## Africa and the WTO

All the African countries except Eritrea, Ethiopia, Somalia, and Sudan are members of the WTO. Negotiations and trade agreements within the WTO concern (cf. Hong Kong, 2005):

—agricultural products: the improvement of access to markets, reduction of internal subsidies with distorting effects, reduction of export subsidies, reduction of consolidated tariffs, and a lack of customs duties on products exported by the Least Developed Countries (LDC);
—non-agricultural products: reduction and elimination of customs duties and tariff peaks, special, differentiated treatment for developing countries;
—services: liberalization in the framework of the General Agreement on Trade in Services (GATS);
—the "Singapore subjects" defined by the WTO: investments, competition, public markets, elimination of obstacles to trade.

Trade liberalization has certain positive effects on African countries, notably by reducing the burden of agricultural

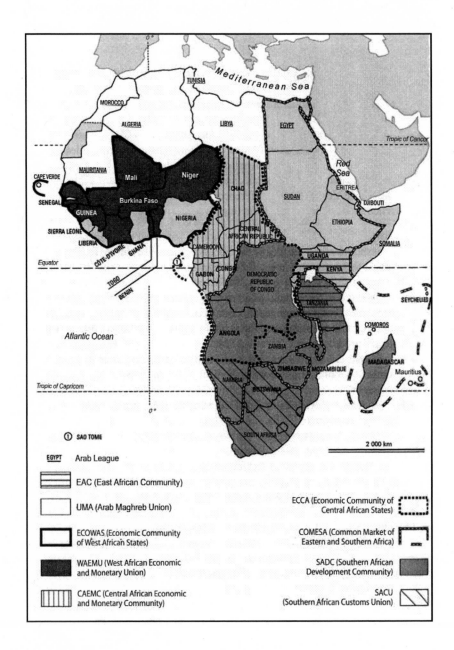

SAO TOME

EGYPT    Arab League

EAC (East African Community)

UMA (Arab Maghreb Union)

ECOWAS (Economic Community
of West African States)

WAEMU (West African Economic
and Monetary Union)

CAEMC (Central African Economic
and Monetary Community)

ECCA (Economic Community of
Central African States)

COMESA (Common Market of
Eastern and Southern Africa)

SADC (Southern African
Development Community)

SACU
(Southern African Customs Union)

subsidies (cf. the Cotton Initiative). In Hong Kong, the WTO decided to eliminate subsidies for agricultural exports in 2006 and for agricultural production in 2013. The Least Developed Countries, unlike emerging countries, are experiencing an erosion of their preferential treatment and their trade margins (cf. the effects of the suppression of the Multifiber Agreement in January 2005 and the suppression of the sugar protocol). Conflicts with the European Union concern meat, cereals, dairy products, and sugar.

## Regionalism and Pan-Africanism

Almost all African countries are engaged in processes of regional integration whose forms range from sectorial cooperation to political union with transfers of sovereignty. Regional integration is a priority for a Balkanized Africa composed of some fifty countries, most of which are small and many of which are enclaves. It is also a political concept that presupposes the establishment of institutional structures and leads to the construction of an identity. It is more or less supported by institutions and commercial arrangements (*de jure* regionalism). It can result, on the contrary, from the practices of actors constituting commercial, financial, cultural, or technological networks in regional spaces, producing a *de facto* regionalism (e.g., African cross-border trade). There are more than 200 regional organizations. The four organizations recognized by the African Union are ECOWAS in West Africa, ECCA in central Africa, SADC in Southern Africa, and COMESA in Eastern Africa.

## Political integration: The African Union and the dream of pan-Africanism

According to a political or diplomatic conception, regional integration involves transfers of sovereignty and goals of preventing conflicts. Convergences of economic interests are a way of moving beyond political rivalries and antagonisms. Transfers of sovereignty and the production of public goods at regional levels are a response to the overwhelming of states in the context of globalization (e.g., the creation of a regional currency). Regional integration presupposes national integration, the strengthening of the state and of citizenship, a strong state preventing territorial fragmentation being based on a strong civil society that creates counter-powers. Processes of regional disintegration are associated with sociopolitical factors of national disintegration and the decomposition of states, with economic and financial crises that give priority to national objectives or to international environments leading to opening *erga omnes* (to the whole world), and with policies pursued at the expense of regional agreements.

The fall of the Berlin Wall and the end of the Cold War have encouraged a preventive diplomacy of managing crises and resolving conflicts within traditional economic organizations.

The New Partnership for Africa's Development (NEPAD) takes a long-term view (ten to fifteen years). It emphasizes the private sector, basing itself on the five main regions of the African Union. It gives priority to Africans' appropriation of the process of development and aims to realize a new partnership founded on shared responsibility and mutual interest. There is supposed to be an examination or pressure by peers. The African Peer Review Mechanism (APRM), the cornerstone of NEPAD and the guarantee of its credibility, has been set up. It is the African countries themselves that must identify, evaluate, and finance common investment projects. However, NEPAD remains a top-down process. The program is very ambitious in comparison with past tendencies and predictions. NEPAD is a process that can be judged only over the long term. It still lacks credibility and legitimacy with regard to the various African states and agents of civil society.

The African Union is getting deeper on the institutional level (with an Assembly, Executive Council, Committee of permanent representatives, and Commission), and is transforming itself into an institution of coordination and integration. The plan of action adopted on 12 October 2004 defines five priorities: 1) institutional transformation, 2) encouragement of peace (Council of Peace and Security), human security, and governance (The African Court of the Rights of Man and Peoples); 3) the promotion of regional integration; 4) the construction of a shared vision within the continent; and 5) the adoption of a protocol relative to the African Union's Court of Justice.

## Economic integration

Regionalization is a process that takes diverse forms (Hugon, 2003). It is characterized by an intensification of movements of exchange with the suppression of internal obstacles (free trade zone), with a common external tariff (customs union), and with a mobility of factors (common market). It may manifest itself in a coordination of economic or social policies (economic union), projects of cooperation set

up by actors (regional or functional cooperation), interdependencies among economies leading to economic convergences (integration of markets), and internalized relations
within networks or firms (productive or reticular integration). It may eventuate in the setting up of rules or a transfer of sovereignty equipped with institutional structures
(institutional integration or federative regionalism).

## Weak regional integration

Spaces that are marginalized with respect to the world
economy are also little integrated regionally and national
disintegration limits regional integration.

Trade among different regions in Africa amounts to about
10 percent of total trade in Africa.. It is focused on a few
countries. Outside South Africa, five countries represent
three-quarters of intra-African exports (Côte d'Ivoire,
Nigeria, Kenya, Zimbabwe, Ghana). Trade within branches
involving manufactured products is very weak; a few basic
products play an important role, oil accounts for a third of
this trade, and cotton, livestock, corn, and cocoa account
for 18 percent. Coordination and unification of monetary
policy are, in the case of the South Africa's Common
Monetary Area (CMA) or the franc zone, at the heart of the
process of regional integration. However, they are absent in
other zones of regional integration and are realized only
indirectly when the member countries in the same zone
have chosen a single anchor for a key currency.

The main factors explaining intra-regional trade are:

—structural factors connected with the level of development (economies trade more among themselves when they
have diversified structures of production and consump-

tion), size, and geographic proximity (in terms of transport and transaction costs), and sociocultural and political proximity (the same currency, language, history);
   —factors of political economy (regional trade agreements, a policy of openness).

On the other hand, the influence of informal trade that creates *de facto* zones of free trade is explained chiefly by:
   —differentials created by borders in terms of political economy and trade regimes;
   —the existence of trade networks and membership in trans-border social networks;
   —economic complementarities and comparative advantages.

This kind of trade is not very integrating insofar as it involves essentially imported transformed products and has more to do with commercial margins than with the creation of added value by transforming products.
   Important progress can be noted, however, in ECOWAS's closer relations with WAEMU, in the SADC under South Africa's influence, and in the East African Community (customs union, common passports, universities).

## Bilateral and Multilateral Cooperation

*Why are you angry with me? I didn't give you anything.*
                                                    —Confucius

Agreements for cooperation and partnership are geopolitical projects involving oil, as well as migratory, military, security, humanitarian, and other issues.

## Aid and cooperation

International cooperation presupposes relationships of mutual exchange and differs from the vertical conception of development aid. It takes place between actors with symmetrical powers. It is situated in a post-colonial context composed of affective ties, guilty consciences, debt not cancelled by the donors, a desire for independence, and a fear of abandonment on the part of the receivers.

When the Berlin Wall fell, aid lost its main geopolitical function. It recovered a significant legitimacy with the insecurity, catastrophes, and conflicts that characterize numerous regions. The conditions set for receiving aid, including good governance and good results, were not well adapted to failed states and weakened regions. Public development aid (PDA) has different motives: humanitarian (emergency aid and the battle against poverty), utilitarian (access to natural resources, presence in protected markets), geostrategic (security, prevention of conflicts, fighting terrorism, management of risks connected with migrations and epidemics, search for a voice in international decision-making), cultural (defense of languages and cultures), moral (post-colonial guilt feelings, white man's burden), and developmentalist (reducing international asymmetries and divergences in itineraries). In a situation in which private funds are drying up, public development aid makes it possible to deal with external financial constraints. Nonetheless, receivers are not always able to absorb aid effectively; it is often diverted away from intended goals and has limited multiplying effects (only about 60 percent of incoming funds are immediately passed on to the general economy). It also produces perverse effects: a bias in favor of capitalistic projects, recurrent expenses (Gabas, 1999).

The Commission for Africa (2005) calls for a "big push" to move beyond the trap of poverty and to do away with subsidies provided by Northern Hemisphere countries, a doubling of aid to Africa, from 25 to 50 billion dollars, between now and 2010, new systems of financing (ease of international financing, an imposed or selective tax on air transportation, etc.), and reports addressed to peoples and no longer solely to money lenders. The International Finance Facility proposed by the United Kingdom would borrow and mobilize large sums of money. However, it would increase the burden on future generations. International taxation, which is recommended by France, has the advantage of being predictable and concessional in character; it can be concentrated on fundamental needs. Wiping the slate clean does not ensure lasting access to international financing, which is hampered, given the lack of structural reforms, by the countries' difficulty in absorbing it. In several countries or fragile regions the problem is conflicts in which the priorities are security and the reconstruction of the state and its minimal sovereign functions by providing the concerted support of the international community. The British Department for International Development (DFID), which has become influential at the World Bank, treats fragile states as a whole and proposes technical solutions aimed at development. It opposes the case-by-case approach adopted by the United States that privileges political criteria (democracy, the fight against terrorism), and is oriented instead toward "good pupils" and security objectives.

## Relations among states

*France and Africa*

Because of its history, France plays the role of a regional power in Africa. As Guirangaud has put it, France thought five hundred men could change Africa's destiny. Several factors explain France's policy with regard to sub-Saharan Africa, where cultural, geopolitical, and humanitarian concerns are dominant, along with certain economic, mining, and oil interests and the support of firms looking for niches. Emphasizing these economic interests does not allow us to understand the complexity of the colonial and post-colonial context. France's political influence in African countries is explained by a multitude of factors: the fear of chaos and a desire to prevent conflicts, a policy of defending the use of the French language, clientele relationships and the constitution of networks for financing French political parties, and the votes that francophone countries have in the United Nations.

Despite the decline in aid (8.2 billion Euros in 2005, or .047 percent of its GDP), France remains one of the primary donors of public development aid—both in absolute numbers and in terms of percentage of GDP. The majority of French aid continues to be directed toward sub-Saharan Africa (55 percent of the total). More than 30 percent of the aid is multilateral. The durability of the networks and of the colonial umbilical cord makes ulterior motives virtually inevitable. Belated de-colonization is a source of resentment.

During the Cold War, France's economic policy with regard to sub-Saharan Africa reflected, in the Gaullist tradition, the geopolitical significance that Paris attached to this region (the French language, UN votes, oil resources, fear of communism). The fall of the Berlin Wall in November 1989, the expansion of Europe, and accelerating globalization led to a decline in Africa's geopolitical importance as well as to a certain normalization of relations between France and Africa. President Mitterand's speech at La Baule in June 1990 (which connected French aid to Africa with democratization, Prime Minister Balladur's 1993 doctrine making bilateral French aid contingent on signing agreements with the Bretton Woods institutions, and the devaluation of the CFA franc in January 1994 were perceived as so many signs indicating that France was cutting Africa loose. The French case-by-case policy, which was on the defensive against the specter of anglophone domination and ambiguous in its talk about countries that were not yet ready for democracy, was criticized by African opinion and governments, especially in Southern Africa. France is both a referee and a player, and sometimes it is caught in the middle (cf. Côte d'Ivoire). The French army acts under the mandate of the United Nations or Europe, but it has maintained its bilateral military agreements with some African countries. *Realpolitik* leads to accommodations with dictators.

In 1950, France's colonial empire accounted for 60 percent of its foreign trade. Africa's share in French exports dropped from 8.7 percent in 1970 to 5 percent in 2006. Africa now provides 4 percent of France's imports. Three countries account for more than 50 percent of French imports from sub-Saharan Africa and 45 percent of French exports to the same area: South Africa, Côte d'Ivoire, and Nigeria. The redeployment of French capital has resulted primarily from interests in oil and a desire to be involved in markets that are more important than those of the francophone countries of Africa.

The franc zone, which was initially established to isolate the French colonial empire from the international market and to create a preferential area after the 1929 crash, has adapted to upheavals as profound as the abandonment of imperial preferences, decolonization, the flexibility of exchange rates, and the convertibility of the French franc. Nor did the franc zone disappear with the devaluation of the CFA franc in 1994 or the introduction of the Euro in 1999. On the other hand, it has evolved. With its devaluation in 1994, the deepening of internal regional integration in the course of the 1990s, the supervision of indicators of convergence within monetary unions, and the implementation of orthodox policies by regional banks that were more independent of political authorities, the monetary unions of Western and central Africa inevitably became less dependent on the French treasury. The introduction of the Euro did not eliminate the ties between the French treasury and central African banks, but it did make them less exclusive and more transparent by increasing the Central European Bank's right of inspection. We also see the two monetary unions, WAEMU and CAEMC, moving in different directions. This development has to do both with changes in the rules of convertibility between the two CFA currencies and the asynchronous situations of the two monetary unions, WAEMU being essentially connected with oil and CAEMC not.

According to the late French president François Mitterand (1957), "Without Africa, there would be no history of France in the twenty-first century." Africa provided French diplomacy and its armed forces the space without which no strategy or power is possible. The agreements and practices adopted when the French Community was established have been maintained, but the links between France and its former colonies have been partly severed. Relations have become tense because of the paternalistic ties of "Franceafrique" (an expression used by Houphouêt Boigny, the first president of Côte d'Ivoire) and numerous points of contention (Rwanda, defense accords, the poor transparency of certain military, oil, and monetary relationships with the franc zone). France has been accused of artificially prolonging the life of autocratic regimes. It is criticized both for intervening and for leaving people to fend for themselves.

Rwanda remains a highly contentious issue between France and Africa. The Hutus were in power when the reconciliation accord between the Hutus and the Tutsis was halted by the death of the Rwandan and Burundian presidents in an air crash. The military machine backing the Hutu government was supported by France. It became genocidal when the assassination of the Rwandan president Habyarimana ignited the tinderbox. The 1994 Rwandan genocide caused a million deaths and two million refugees.

Relations between France and Côte d'Ivoire grew tense after an Ivoirian air attack caused the death of eight French soldiers in 2004. France destroyed Côte d'Ivoire's air force, and the violent demonstrations in Côte d'Ivoire led to the departure of 8,000 French citizens.

The French maintained a considerable military presence in Africa in 2007 (6,000 men in Côte d'Ivoire, Djibouti, Gabon, Senegal, Central African Republic, and Chad), not counting the 3,000 men involved in Operation Licorne, which has been reduced in scope since the Ougadougou accords of March 4, 2007, or the limited interventions carried out under European or United Nations command. France's military bases, established in accord with defense agreements, are located in Côte d'Ivoire, Djibouti, Gabon, Central African Republic, and Senegal. The Reinforcement of African Peacekeeping Capacities Program (RECAMP), which provides training and support for African military forces, is supposed to be Europeanized, and French forces are to be refocused on Senegal, Gabon, and Djibouti. France's military interventions seek to secure oil production, establish a protective barrier preventing domino effects (e.g., support for the Central African Republic and Chad in 2006, reversing former prime minister Lionel Jospin's doctrine of non-intervention).

Almost three thousand French troops with a large arsenal of weapons are stationed at the French military base in Djibouti, with maritime and aerial surveillance from the outpost on the Red Sea. The "battle against terrorism" has led to the establishment of American military bases (Combined Joint Task Force-Horn of Africa, CJTF-HOA, a coalition of eleven countries consisting of 85 percent American Marines and Special Forces), and to the presence of British, German, Spanish, and Japanese troops. This "military switching yard" makes it possible to carry out naval and air surveillance of Al-Qaeda's activities along the coasts of Yemen, Somalia, and Kenya, as well as operations in the Persian Gulf and the Red Sea, where one-fourth of the world's oil transport takes place. French military forces are supposed ultimately to be regrouped in Dakar, Libreville, and Djibouti.

Many questions remain with the election of Nicolas Sarkozy as president of the republic in May 2007. Will the African policies of De Gaulle, Mitterand, and Chiraq be continued? Should France withdraw from Africa or at least normalize its relations with a continent marked by distant, complex, and even insoluble crises? Or should it reassert its presence in view of new strategic stakes relating to access to natural resources, the presence of new powers (the United States, China, and India), the management of environmental or epidemiological interdependencies, and the threat of contagion represented by terrorist networks in the Sudan-Sahel region and in the Horn of Africa? Should France maintain a *realist* African policy through military bases, diplomacy based on long-term alliances, fighting fanaticism, and adopting a line of conduct that is at once autonomous and responsible with regard to its American and European allies and the "battle against China's attempt to buy Africa in defiance of any moral or political consideration" (Bernard Kouchner)? Should it transfer basic prerogatives to Europe (in the monetary, military, and diplomatic areas)? Should it, on the contrary, adopt a "transformational diplomacy," with a duty to intervene on behalf of suffering peoples, to exert pressure for democratic change, and to defend human rights?

## The United States and Africa

The remark that "Africa is more a European problem than an American problem" is less valid today. The direct ties are old, notably those connecting Afro-Americans to Liberia. During the Cold War, American policy was chiefly anti-Soviet. After the events in Somalia, the United States sought to avoid casualties and economic interests prevailed. President Clinton's policy had three main objectives: finding African solutions to African problems, bringing Africa into global economic circuits, and opposing Islamist terror-ism (Libya, Sudan). Since September 11, 2001, American policy has become activist again. Its three priorities are: 1) the battle against terrorism and strengthening the strategy of containing Islamism through a program of military assis-tance; 2) increasing trade and investments in oil (American imports from Africa were to rise from 15 percent in 2001 to 25 percent by 2020), American firms being present notably in Somaliland, southern Sudan, the countries of the Sahel and the Gulf of Guinea; and 3) the development of trade and aid based on liberalism. The United States relies on piv-otal states that have regulatory capacities. It also seeks to respond to so-called asymmetrical risks (conflicts within countries, failing states that have problems with traffickers or terrorists, or where technical ability is insufficient). Thus it is developing democracy and the market by relying on civilians—"civilianization." "Shaping" is a preventive defense that shapes the environment by diffusing American norms, values, and standards. Bilateralism permitting a case-by-case approach and privileging friends in the axis of good is dominant, even if today's friends may be tomor-row's enemies.

The African Growth and Opportunity Act (AGOA) seeks to favor trade between Africa and the United States, which is currently limited. This initiative concerns chiefly oil and to a lesser extent textiles. Thirty-six African countries are officially eligible, depending on certain criteria: achieving continuous progress toward a market economy, respecting the law, free trade, and adopting policies that reduce pover-ty and increase protection for worker's rights. The United States has increased its ideological activities as well as its military and diplomatic presence.

In 2002, the Americans established bases in Diego Garcia and Djibouti (with the end of the French preserve) and plan others in Sao Tomé. They are also trying to respond to so-called "asymmetrical" risks (conflicts within states or failing states where traffickers and terrorists are active and technological superiority does not provide sufficient control). They have set up an African section within the Unified Command Plan. They are supporting the forces fighting Islamist radicalism, but by often confusing Islamics with Islamists they may also be contributing to this radicalism (cf. their support for Ethiopia's intervention in Somalia in 2006 and 2007). The Horn of Africa is strategically important (oil transport, Islamist radicalism). The United States plans to create a Sixth Army for Africa (Africom) both to protect oil transportation (in the Gulf of Guinea and via the Chad-Cameroon and Higling-Sudanese ports) and to monitor radical Islamist networks that might be set up in the failing states that provide sanctuaries for Al-Qaeda. The Americans have suffered diplomatic and military setbacks in Darfur, where they are confronted by the influence of Libya, China, and the Arab League.

## Great Britain and Africa

Great Britain has a long African tradition, but it has not had a true African policy since African countries became independent. Its African policy was diluted in the ties linking it to members of the Commonwealth. The latter received most British aid, which was concentrated on Nigeria and South Africa. After Tony Blair took office in 1997, there was a fundamental change in British policy. The military intervention in Sierra Leone in May 2000 marked a turning point. Opposition to Mugabe passed through Common-wealth channels. Foreign policy has been given an ethical content alongside *Realpolitik*. The role of civil society and the churches is important in this new policy, and is now being reinforced around two main axes: the policy of coop-eration and an increase in aid (cf. the Commission for Africa's International Finance Facility, which provides for an increase of 25 billion dollars in aid in the form of a loan reimbursed by the G-7 nations with the help of NEPAD). Africa is appearing as a major strategic stake on the geopo-litical level, with the Least Developed Nations group having priority. British policy reconciles global ethics, self-interest, and the principles of economic liberalism.

## The European Union and Africa

In its relations with Africa, the European Union differen-tiates between Southern Africa (free-trade agreements) and the countries in the Africa-Caribbean-Pacific (ACP) zone (the Cotonou Convention). The four axes are peace and security, governance, commercial integration and com-merce, and development.

The European Union is not a power that has internation-al sovereignty or a military intervention force of its own, despite the European policy of sovereignty and defense. It accepts Atlanticism and the role of NATO. It intervenes in Africa through partnership, multilateralism, diplomacy in the area, and soft power.

On the level of trade and development, the Yaoundé and Lomé accords between the European Community and the ACP countries are situated in a regionalist perspective of preferences and non-reciprocity that takes international asymmetries into account. They seek to bring the former colonies in Africa, the Caribbean, and the Pacific into preferential agreements with their old mother-countries that are joining the European sphere. They have lost much of their legitimacy and strength with the expansion of Europe to countries with no colonial past and with the reorientation of interests toward Eastern Europe since the fall of the Berlin wall. Adjustment has led the doctrines of the money lenders to converge under the leadership of the Bretton Woods Institutions. The European Union, speaking with a single voice in the WTO, has put its agreements in conformity with the WTO's rules. The observed results of the Lomé accords are ambivalent. The sugar protocol and industrial preferences have favored the industrialization of Mauritius, thanks to a productive allocation of sugar revenues. The preferences established by the Lomé accords have served as a catalyst and led to expansion and diversification in countries such as Kenya, Mauritius, and Zimbabwe. Aid in the form of gifts has made it possible to make secure sectors considered to have priority, especially in the area of infrastructure, health, and food supply. But these preferences have not been a sufficient or perhaps even necessary condition. African countries have not been able to maintain their market shares or to diversify their production, even though they have had free access to the European market for 95 percent of agricultural exports. The principles of non-reciprocity and discrimination among developing countries and the Lomé accords were in relative contradiction with the WTO's rules.

The Cotonou Convention calls for free-trade agreements and economic partnership agreements that could substitute for the system of general preferences or preferences granted to the Least Developed Countries in the context of the European Union's "anything but weapons" program, which calls for preferential rules for all products with the exception of weapons. The economic partnership agreements between the European Union and the ACP countries or regional groups are to be set up between 2008 and 2020.

The European Union's intervention has three parts: preventive diplomacy, the military management of wars, and peaceful resolution of conflicts. Since December 2003 it has adopted common foreign and security policies. The European constitutional treaty, which has not been ratified, foresaw a stronger institutional apparatus (a minister of foreign affairs, a president of the European Council, an increased role for the European parliament). The European Council has privileged ties with the African Union and regional organizations. The European Union finances logistical support, training for police forces and armies, disarmament and demobilization. Thus it is present in Ituri with Operation Artemis, in the Democratic Republic of the Congo, in Sudan, in Somalia, and in West Africa. The transfer of security to the European Union (e.g., the RECAMP program) makes it possible to decolonialize bilateral relations between former mother countries and colonies.

European policies in the areas of commerce, agriculture, and development lack coherence. They remain largely dependent on those of the member states. The expansion of the European Union has taken place at the expense of an African policy. In contrast to its openness to the former countries of Eastern Europe, Europe continues to lack an ambitious policy with regard to Africa—despite the historical and geographical proximities, at least for Southern Europe. Need it be recalled that the structural funds accorded the ten new countries entering the European Union represent, per capita and per annum, more than 500 Euros, whereas fewerthan 15 Euros are accorded African countries?

## Asia and Africa

Relations among African and Asian countries depend on trade networks and Asian diasporas. They are being transformed by the rise in the power of these Asian emergent countries, which represent one third of the world population and have considerable needs for raw materials.

Japan's relations with Africa have long been limited to trade, investment, and aid, in order to be present in markets and to gain access to raw materials. Excepting South Africa, Japan's trade with Africa represents less than 2 percent of its foreign trade. With the Tokyo International Conference on African Development (TICAD), where there were discussions on cooperation with Japan, Asia, and Africa, there has been a strong emphasis on relations and the objectives of stability and peace have become more important. Japanese aid to Africa is increasing and in many anglophone countries, Japan is the major donor. Japan wants to present itself as a model providing an alternative to the Washington Consensus (cf. the financing of the "East Asian Miracle"). Its growing presence in Africa is also connected with its rivalry with China.

India, whose economic growth is close to that of China (7 percent per annum), is less a regional than an emergent national power, thanks to the size of its population, its strong growth, its performance in high technology sectors, and its military arsenal. It is present in Africa especially through the networks of the Indian diaspora in East Africa and the Indian Ocean, but also in the domain of oil. It is positioning itself in the service and the high-technology branches, while at the same time developing cooperation, especially with regard to oil. Its practices are in no way inferior to those of China.

Relations between China and Africa are essentially economic and are based on the win-win principle. Sino-African trade doubled between 2000 and 2004, and in 2007 it should exceed Africa's trade with the United States (50 billion dollars in 2006). China needs raw materials and especially oil; thus it has established ties with South Africa, Angola, Gabon, Niger, Nigeria, and Sudan (which explains its vote in the UN Security Council regarding Darfur). China is the world's second largest consumer of oil, and Africa provides 25 percent of its supplies. China finds African market outlets in the areas of public works, telecommunications, and textiles. Its balance of trade with Africa is slightly in deficit. Its exports to Africa amount to more than 15 billion dollars, more than half of which is for products with high added value (machines, electronics, new technologies). The abolition of the multifiber accords has caused China's textile exports to explode, providing strong competition for companies in South Africa, Mauritius, Madagascar, Morocco, and Tunisia. It is investing in joint ventures worth more than a billion dollars and associating Western technology with economic advantages connected with low Chinese costs and government subsidies (cf. telecommunications). China's aid for Africa is multiple, and virtually without counterpart—it insists only that Taiwan not be recognized— and is growing at a rapid pace. One of China's priorities is to ensure the security of trade routes and oil supplies; Djibouti, which controls the old route to the Indies, is one of the support points. However, on the whole economic relationships remain post-colonial, except with South Africa. Africa exports raw materials, while China exports manufactured products.

Relations between China and Africa are political, and testify to pragmatism and *Realpolitik*. China has a major policy of cultural cooperation. It is training 10,000 Africans in China. Relationships are formed outside international rules (zero-interest credit and the role of Chinese public companies that are connected with the state and the party). China, which absorbs 60 percent of the citrus fruit exported by Africa, does not respect, in the name of the priority of economic development, environmental norms. China uses its eminent position in the United Nations to protect its friends and develop a third-world ideology of countries without a colonial past. This allows many countries to evade international sanctions (as in the cases of Zimbabwe and Sudan). Cooperation means that the principle of non-interference and the sovereignty of states prevails over that of human rights. It can be said that Chinese arms sales and support for certain rogue states have helped feed armed conflicts in Africa (Angola, Ethiopia, Sudan).

China has greatly increased its military relationships with Africa, in the form of cooperation with African military powers (e.g., South Africa), in direct opposition to Western interests (e.g., Sudan), and in connection with flexible diplomacy (e.g., Nigeria). Sino-African military cooperation led in 2006 to visits by Chinese military delegations or political officials to Algeria, Tunisia, South Africa, Namibia, Sudan, and Tanzania, where they signed official military agreements. Chinese arms sales and support for certain "rogue states" could be said to have helped feed armed conflicts in Africa (Angola, Ethiopia, Sudan, Chad). China has become a provider of weapons to states and to various guerrilla movements. This strategy is pursued through official relations, state-controlled companies, and unofficial networks. However, in order to have an enduring presence, China is obliged to have a pragmatic policy and to take into account criticisms made within Africa and by international authorities. In 2007, it also issued statements regarding the environment and peace in Darfur.

## The Iberian Peninsula and Africa

Spain had few colonies in Africa other than Equatorial Guinea, which is now a member of the Central African Economic and Monetary Community. Its role in Africa has been minor in comparison with its role in Latin America. Portugal, on the other hand, was the first and the last colonizer in Africa. Decolonization was achieved through wars of great violence in Angola, Guinea-Bissau, and Mozambique. Portugal plays an important role in its ex-colonies where Portuguese is still spoken (Angola, Cape Verde, Guinea-Bissau, Mozambique, Sao Tomé and Principe).

## Russia and Africa

During the Cold War, the USSR pursued an active strategy with regard to Africa as part of its battle against "imperialists and capitalists" by supporting so-called socialist African states and opposition forces connected with the communist party. About 100,000 Africans received training in the USSR. Russian technical assistance and military support were notable in many "socialist" countries (Mali,

Guinea, Madagascar, etc.). During apartheid, there were important links between the African National Congress, the main South African party opposing apartheid, and the USSR.

However, after the fall of communism and of apartheid at the end of the 1980s, these ties became much looser. Since 2005 a change in the geopolitical situation of both South Africa and Russia has taken place that may suggest the beginning of a strategic alliance. Both countries are currently benefiting from the mining boom. Russia has significant influence in Africa (cf. Russia's Security Council abstention regarding Darfur). South Africa is seeking Russian support for a seat on the United Nations Security Council. Russian mining, gas, and oil oligopolies are active in South Africa, Angola, Gabon, Ghana, Guinea, Nigeria, and the Democratic Republic of the Congo. Russia, which has been absent from the African scene for the past fifteen years, needs support and greater visibility, if only to counter the growing ties between Africa and emerging countries such as India and especially China. The renewal of ties between Russia and Africa is significant. Henceforth, we will probably have to expect a new actor to be present in Africa alongside the Western powers and emergent countries such as Brazil, India, and China.

## Latin America and Africa

The ties between Latin America and Africa, which are anchored in the memory of slavery, underwent numerous transformations after independence. Cuba played an important role during the Cold War by supporting front-line states (in Southern Africa) and, in conjunction with the

USSR, socialist countries. Today, new situations are leading to a role for emerging countries, and especially Brazil. Brazil has acknowledged its slavery-debt to Africa, has close relationships with Portuguese-speaking countries, and wants to play, along with South Africa, a growing role in the international architecture.

Africa's relationships are obviously more diversified. Those with Brazil are growing, and those with Russia have been decreasing since 1989, except in the new triangular trade..

## Non-governmental international relations

The United States remains, to be sure, the superpower on the world chessboard, proposing a global model and using both hard power—notably military—and soft power to control new instruments of power such as technology, communication, information, trade, and finance. But contrary to realist theories, new actors have appeared on the international scene and are playing a growing role, whether in private firms or in NGOs. The anti-globalization movement is reawakening a certain unity among the excluded that might strengthen the unity of Southern Hemisphere countries.

### Decentralized cooperation and territorial collectivities

Decentralized cooperation involves chiefly territorial collectivities and organizations of international solidarity. It has numerous advantages of proximity, reducing transaction costs and rates of evaporation between the sums expended and the sums that are made available to end-users. Decentralization is a mode of institutional organization that consists in the management of the affairs peculiar to a territorial collectivity by elective deliberative organs with the participation of civil society. It differs from decon-centration, a simple mode of administrative organization consisting in transferring responsibilities and the attributes of central power to local authorities. In many African coun-tries, local authorities lack means and shift responsibility for most urban services (water, electricity, roads, security, waste disposal, transportation, etc.) either to the private sector, where the population is solvent, or to NGOs or associations for the poorest people. Decentralization is combined with privatization and the rise of associations for meeting collec-tive needs.

Decentralized cooperation collides with asymmetries of power and organizational capacity among collectivities of the northern and southern hemispheres. Decentralization is not local democracy. The former can lead to power being held by notables or oligarchs, whereas the latter implies counter-powers and public debate.

*The role of international solidarity*
*and humanitarian action organizations*

Confronted by the failures of governments and the com-plexity of bilateral or multilateral aid, organizations of inter-national solidarity and humanitarian action are playing an increasing role as lobbies affecting public opinion, affecting both the agendas of international negotiations and emer-gency interventions. The impulses of generosity and solidar-ity testify to the emergence of a sense of transnational citi-zenship. NGOs act rapidly and largely fill gaps left by offi-cial cooperation. NGOs' net annual donations are estimated to be seven billion dollars annually, or 14 percent of public development aid. But the road to hell is paved with good intentions. How can one keep the rags collected by these organizations from threatening the textile industry, or free distribution of drugs from conflicting with the process of developing generic drugs or the recovering cost of drugs already on the market (the Bamako initiative)? In some cases, the multiplicity of projects is outside a fixed framework and the priorities announced by public policies. Questions of coordination and legitimacy arise between NGOs and territorial collectivities (e.g., communes), between the latter and regions, between the regional level and the national level, and between the national level and the European or multi-national level.

*Africa in networks*

The great formal and informal networks are connected with international circuits. They are multiple. The circulation of people, goods, and information is carried out between the coasts of Eastern Africa and the Arabian Peninsula, given life by air transport and telecommunications (Dubai Street in Zanizibar). In Southern Africa, communities of Indian merchants are reviving the commerce of the islands of Southeast Asia. Migrants from West Africa participate in European migratory networks. Murid proselytism has many contacts with North America. Nigerian Ibo networks control a significant share of the drug trade in New York City.

*Africa and global public goods*

Intergovernmental relations are overwhelmed by the global scale, whether in the area of financial stabilization, atmospheric pollution, water management, epidemiological risks, or security and the battle against terrorism. There is no supra-national authority that has the legitimacy required to produce and finance these goods, hence there is a less than optimal production of world public goods. We can resort to the distinction between goods at the disposal of elites (e.g., scientific knowledge), those that depend on weak areas (e.g., terrorism or epidemics) and additive goods (e.g., $CO_2$). In the case of Africa, chiefly the second type of goods is concerned (Gabas, Hugon 2003).

# Geopolitical Perspectives and Prospects for Africa

*Winds are favorable only for those who know where they're going.*                                                    —Seneca

The temporality of globalization (competitiveness, openness, adaptation to new conditions, etc.) is not the same as that of economic development (in terms of the establishment of institutions, construction of markets, sustainable progress in productivity) or that of the sociohistorical trajectories of African societies (the construction of nation-states, redefinition of borders, and the double, internal and external legitimation of powers). These different Africas are constructing their own modernity by combining their own historical temporalities with the temporality of modernization. But how can these different temporalities be reconciled in order to encourage a negotiated globalization and to control opening?

*Africa, a new strategic stake*

After the fall of the Berlin Wall, European eyes and European capital have tended to turn toward the East. Africa is no longer a stake in an ideological bidding war, as it had been during the Cold War. This does not mean—quite the contrary—that diplomatic rivalries and factional battles supported by foreign powers came to an end. The rise in tensions and conflicts is all the greater because the economic stakes are more concerned with the appropriation of natural resources (e.g., diamonds or oil) and control over trafficking (contraband, drugs) than with gaining access to markets. Africa has become strategic once again for reasons of security, because of its raw materials and its biodiversity. The importance of oil and the environment is increasing. Fear alternates with a desire for protection, for taking responsibility, for interfering to avoid catastrophes, and even for development projects. Africa's problems can have a boomerang effect in the form of migratory flows, epidemics, the exportation of violence, and disintegrated states that provide sanctuaries for terrorists.

*Numerous internal challenges*

Crisis, rupture, and mutation have accentuated the ambiguity of an Africa that already showed many contrasts. It is difficult to discern the events that will construct a future "that approaches on turtle doves' feet" (Nietzsche) and the significant facts that will cause one of the many possible paths to become history. With hindsight we can see that the pessimism about Asia that was dominant a few decades ago was ill-founded. Development is sometimes a matter of generations.

African societies have to deal with a doubling of their population and a tripling of their urban population between now and 2025. They have to reconstitute their ecosystems, make the collective and productive investments necessary for growth, and position themselves in the international labor market. These various challenges imply increases in productivity and long-term capital accumulation. Harvests have to be doubled and productivity tripled over the next twenty-five years. It is imperative to respond to the challenges of population pressure, urban growth, the exposure of protected agriculture to competition, liberalization, and the magnitude of environmental risks. In societies in which the nation-state is still being constructed and personal networks and ethnic solidarities are more important than the institutionalization of the state, the economic crisis has increased the latter's disintegration. In a few extreme cases, it has transformed a revenue economy into a criminal, plundering economy. When that happens, the future of the state is the future of the economy.

*Contrasting perspectives on integration into the global economy*

The evolution of Africa will remain largely dependent on its place in the international architecture and the world economy. The latter will be reflected in an increase in the power of the immaterial economy and technologies of information, of the technological and institutional environment, in the ability to attract investments, and in competitiveness connected with the quality of products and with logistics. Most simulations predict growing divergences between Europe and Africa because of threshold effects and the effects of agglomeration and larger profits in industrial countries. Africa may benefit from decreasing costs (e.g., for computers or Internet access), make technological leaps forward, or find new competitive markets. The efficiency of new technologies depends on the social, economic, and technical fabric that allows them to be appropriated.

*Strategic options, the stakes, and the role of actors*

Uncontrolled explosions or brushfires can be propagated by a few sparks unless proactive action is taken. Depending on the strategy adopted, a handicap can be a challenge or an asset, as is shown by the example of population pressures on the high plateaus in Kenya and the Bamileke region of Cameroon. In the same way, an asset can become a handicap; the curse of oil in Nigeria, Chad, Equatorial Guinea, Angola, and the Democratic Republic of the Congo is a conclusive example of this. As A. Hirschmann (1958) said, development consists in "tacking back and forth to hold the chosen course by using favorable and contrary winds." The question is how to manage different tempos. Thus a policy indispensable for controlling fecundity will have significant effects only after fifteen years have elapsed.

The actors who will have great impact on Africa's development are in part outside Africa (international institutions, former colonial powers, trans-national companies, diasporic networks, etc.). However, most of them are fundamentally internal. Will mercantile capital be converted into productive capital? Will microproducers become small entrepreneurs with the development of a network linking small and middle-sized enterprises with small and middle-sized industries? Strategies of positive integration into the world economy presuppose new alliances that privilege productive capital and investment at risk. This is possible in the short term only by slashing revenues that are often factors of sociopolitical equilibrium and by freeing entrepreneurs from social and political constraints. Will military conflicts be factors in forming states and recomposing territories and ethnic, familial, and clan identities, Africa being left to its own historical development, or, on the contrary, will wars have to be analyzed in relation to a process of integration into a wheeler-dealer or even criminal economy that disintegrates the state and citizenship?

*Geopolitical scenarios*

Three geopolitical scenarios can be distinguished in relation to these major tendencies and the actors' strategic options:

• The scenario of an Africa out of synch with global time

In terms of Fernand Braudel's *longue durée*, there is a parenthesis corresponding to colonization and modernization, the long time needed to manage the challenges that industrialized societies have spent centuries mastering, and the impossibility of positive insertion into a world organized outside Africa. African historical trajectories are characterized by the dynamics of population, transformations in the way space is occupied, territorial reconfigurations, and changes in the borders inherited from colonialization. This scenario can be played out politically in a positive way (war makes the state, which recomposes itself) or a negative way (left to itself, Africa tears itself apart and states disintegrate). It can be played out economically in a positive way (the dynamism of the popular economy, satisfaction of basic needs, a desired disconnection, endogenization) or a negative way (involuntary disconnection, failure of modernity, a predatory economy, and even entropic chaos with respect to which the community remains passive).

• The scenario of an Africa positively integrated into globalization

The insertion of Africa into a world economy can be achieved through commercial or financial circuits, or even through privatized capital accumulation achieved through illegal activities. It can also result from liberal reforms that have been internalized by the actors. Africa, thanks to its new generations, becomes competitive, productive, democratic. Citizenship and a democratic system develop. The economy is driven from the outside with an acceleration of exports and attractiveness for investment and a growing connection with a network of small and middle-sized enterprises and industries forming a basic economic fabric. This scenario presupposes that Africa has a voice in the international architecture and access to external financing for progress in productivity. It implies a return to saving and to the competencies of Africans working outside Africa. It implies external support, notably by Europe, in commercial and financial terms. A productive, competitive economy implies the mobilization of national and foreign competencies and the emergence of entrepreneurs. This in turn presupposes a favorable institutional framework, a state that acts as a facilitator, a climate of confidence, and a return to security. However, this scenario risks being exclusive and leading to continued poverty among the masses, at least in the short and medium term.

• The scenario of Africas differentiated around regional centers

Great regional powers such as South Africa and Nigeria emerge. Reconfigurations are made around these centers. Insertion into the world economy is highly differentiated depending on the country and the region. A dual Africa is possible, a "useful" Africa and an "excluded" Africa that correspond to growing territorial and social differences. The maintenance of external revenues, the prevention of conflicts, and the exploitation of mining resources are assured. Confronted by growing numbers, confined in structures, the population resorts to an informal economy, living and surviving in a universe of poverty and precariousness. This intermediary scenario may bifurcate into one of the two preceding ones.

There will probably be growing differentiation between African societies. Agro-pastoral priorities are not the same for the nomadic economies of the Tuaregs, gatherers in the equatorial forests, or peasants on the Madagascar highlands. The choice between an economy that is open to the outside or one that is turned inward differs for small coastal countries and large countries. Management of self-sufficiency and alimentary security poses radically different problems in small, overpopulated islands than it does in large countries where land is abundant. The enclaved countries of the Sahel and countries at war are in danger of being marginalized. Countries that export agricultural products will experience an impoverishing specialization if they do not diversify their exports. Countries receiving mining and oil revenues will run the risk of misfortune and instability if they do not manage these revenues.

History has no meaning; there are histories to which people give meaning.

# NOTES

1. In the tradition of Las Casas, who condemned the massacre of the Amerindians, and in that of the Enlightenment.

2. See, for example, Hegel's conception of Africa as a continent in its childhood, and Malthus's view of Africa as illustrating the three Fates (wars, epidemics, famines).

3. André Gide, *Voyage au Congo*.

4. De Gaulle, *Mémoires d'espoir*.

5. Cf. the role played by Mgr. Tutu in South Africa when apartheid was ending or by the Catholic and Protestant churches in Madagascar during the 2001 crisis.

6. Cf. the South African Truth and Reconciliation Commission and the accords signed in Rwanda, Burundi, and Sudan.

7. An extensive irrigation system built in 1932.

# REFERENCES

## Books and Periodicals

Amselle, J.-L., and E. M'Bokolo, 1999. *Au coeur de l'ethnie. Ethnie, tribalisme et État en Afrique.* Paris, La Découverte (1st ed. 1985).

Anda, M. O., 2000. *International Relations in Contemporary Africa.* New York, University Press of America.

Bach, D., and E. Kirk-Green, 1995. *États et sociétés en Afrique francophone.* Paris, Economica.

Balandier, G., 1967. *Anthropologie politique.* Paris, PUF.

Banégas, R., 2003. *La démocratie à pas de camélion. Transition et imaginaires politiques au Bénin.* Paris, Karthala.

Bayart, J.-F., B. Hibou, and C. Ellis, 1997. *La criminalisation des États en Afrique.* Brussels, Éditions Complexe.

Bessis, S., 2003. *L'Occident et les autres.* Paris, La Découverte.

Bohannan, P., and G. Dalton, 1962. *Markets in Africa.* Chicago, Northwestern University Press.

Bourmaud, D., 1997. *La politique en Afrique.* Paris, Montchrestien.

Brunel, S., 2004. *L'Afrique: un continent en réserve de développement.* Rosny-sous-Bois, Bréal.

Chataigner, J.-M., 2004. "Aide publique au développement et réformes des systèmes de sécurité," *Afrique contemporaine*, AFD, no. 209. Paris, La documentation française.

Chrétien, J.-P., and G. Prunier, 2003. *Les ethnies ont une histoire.* Paris, Karthala.

Clapham, C., 2001. *Africa in the International System. The Politics of State Survival.* Cambridge, Cambridge University Press.

Cling, J.-P., M. Razafindrakoto, and F. Roubaud, 2003. *Les nouvelles stratégies de lutte contre la pauvreté.* Paris, Karthala.

Collier, P., and A. Hoeffler, 2000. "On Economic Causes of Civil Wars," *Oxford Economic Papers* 50: 563-573, Oxford, Oxford University Press.

Commission pour l'Afrique, 2005. *Notre intérêt commun. Rapport de la commission pour l'Afrique.* London.

Copans, J., 1990. *La longue marche de la modernité africaine.* Paris,

Karthala.

Coquery-Vidrovitch, C., 1992. *Afrique noire. Permanences et ruptures*. Paris, L'Harmattan.

Coulon, C., and P.-C. Martin, 1991. *Les Afriques politiques*. Paris, La Découverte.

Cour, J.-M., 2000. *Étude des perspectives à long terme de l'Afrique de l'Ouest. Pour penser l'avenir de l'Afrique de l'Ouest*. Paris, OCDE, Club du Sahel.

Courade, G., 2006. *L'Afrique des idées reçues*. Paris, Belin.

Coussy, J., and J. Vallin, 1996. *Crise et population en Afrique*. CEPED, Paris.

Damon, J., and J. Igué, 2003. *L'Afrique de l'Ouest dans la compétition mondiale*. Paris, Karthala.

De Melo, J., and A. Panagariya, 1996. *New Dimensions in Regional Integration*. Cambridge, Cambridge University Press.

Dubresson, A., and J.-P. Raison, 2003. *L'Afrique subsaharienne: une géographie du changement*. 2nd ed. Paris, Armand Colin.

Dunn, K. C., and T. M. Shaw, 2001. *Africa's Challenge to International Relations Theory*. New York, Palgrave.

*Esprit*, 2005. "Vues d'Afrique," no. 317 (August-September). Paris, Esprit.

Fassin, D., 2006. *Quand les corps se souviennent. Expériences et politiques du sida en Afrique du Sud*. Paris, La Découverte.

Ferguson, J., 1990. *The Anti-politics Machine. Development, Depoliticization and Bureaucratic Power in Lesotho*. Minneapolis, University of Minnesota Press.

Fortes, M., and E. Evans-Pritchard, 1940. *African Political Systems*. Oxford, Oxford University Press.

Gabas, J.-J., 1999. *Quel espace de coopération entre l'Europe et les pays ACP?* Paris, GEMDEV, Karthala.

Gabas, J.-J., and P. Hugon, 2001. "Les biens publics mondiaux et la coopération internationale," *L'Économie politique*, no. 12. Paris, Alternatives Économiques.

GEMDEV, 1999. *La mondialisation: les mots et les choses*. Paris, Karthala.

Giri, J., 1986. *L'Afrique noire en panne: vingt-cinq ans de développement*. Paris, Karthala.

Gluckman, M., 1963. *Order and Rebellion in Tribal Africa*. New York, Free Press of Glencoe.

Gourou, P., 1991. *L'Afrique tropicale, nain ou géant agricole?* Paris, Flammarion.

Hirschman, A. O., 1958. *Stratégie du développement économique*. Paris, Éditions Ouvrières.

Hugon, P., 1997. *Économie politique internationale et mondialisation*. Paris, Economica.

Hugon, P., 1999. *La zone franc à l'heure de l'euro*. Paris, Karthala.

Hugon, P., 2003. *Les économies en développement à l'heure de la régionalisation*. Paris, Karthala.

Hugon, P., 2006. *L'économie de l'Afrique*. 5th ed. Paris, La Découverte.

Hugon, P., J. Coussy, and O. Sudrie, 1989. *Urbanisation et dépendance alimentaire en Afrique subsaharienne*. Paris, SEDES.

Hugon, P., and C.-A. Michalet, 2005. *Les nouvelles régulations de l'économie mondiale*. Paris, Kartha.

Hugon, P., G. Pourcet, and S. Quiers-Valette, 1994. *L'Afrique des incertitudes*. Paris, PUF.

Hugon, P., and O. Sudrie, 2000. *Un Bilan de la prospective africaine*. 3 vols. Paris, Rapport MAE/CERED, series "Études."

Illife, J., 2002. *Africans. The History of a Continent*. Cambridge, Cambridge University Press.

Jean, F., and J.-C. Ruffin, 1996. *Économie des guerres civiles*. Paris, Hachette.

Kabout, A., 2001. *Et si l'Afrique refusait le développement?* Paris, l'Harmattan.

Kaldor, M., 1999. *New and Old Wars: Organized Violence in a Global Era*. Oxford, Polity Press.

Keller, E.-J. and D. Rothchild, 1996. *Africa in the International Order*. Boulder, Colorado, Lynne Riener Press.

Ki-Zerbo, J., 1998. *Histoire de l'Afrique noire*. Paris, Hatier.

Ki-Zerbo, J., 2003. *À quand l'Afrique?* Paris, Éditions de l'Aube.

Kourouma, A., 2000. *Allah n'est pas obligé*. Paris, Le Seuil.

Mahieu, R., 1990. *Les fondements de la crise économique en Afrique*. Paris, L'Harmattan.

Maquet, J., 1970. *Pouvoir et société en Afrique*. Paris, Hachette.

Mbembe, A., 2000. *On the Postcolony*. Berkeley, University of California Press.

M'Bokolo, E., 2004. *Afrique noire, histoire et civilisations*, vols. 2-3. Paris, Hatier.

Médart, J.-F., 1992. *États d'Afrique noire: formations, mécanismes et crises*. Paris, Karthala.

Meillassoux, C., 1974. *Femmes, greniers et capitaux*. Paris, Maspero.

Michailof, S., 1993. *La France et l'Afrique: vade-mecum pour un nouveau voyage*. Paris, Karthala.

Ngoupandé, J.-P., 2002. *L'Afrique sans la France. Histoire d'un divorce consommé*. Paris, Albin Michel.

North, D., 1990. *Institutions, Institutional Change and Economic Performances*. New York, Cambridge University Press.

Oliver de Sardan, J.-P., 1995. *Anthropologie et développement: essai en socio-anthropologie du changement social*. Paris, Karthala.

Palan, R., 1998. "Les fantômes du capitalisme mondial: l'économie politique internationale et l'école française de la régulation." *L'Année de la Régulation*, 2. Paris, Presses de Sciences Politiques.

Pétré-Grenouilleau, O., 2005. *Les traites négrières*. Paris, Gallimard.

Pourtier, R., 2001. *Afriques noires*. Paris, Hachette.

Raffinot, M., and J.-Y. Moisseron, 2000. *Dette et pauvreté*. Paris, Economica.

Sall, A., 2000. *La compétitivité future des économies africaines*. Paris, Karthala.

Sall, A., 2003. *Afrique 2025: quels futurs possibles pour l'Afrique au sud du Sahara?* Paris, Karthala.

Sellier, J., 2003. *Atlas des peuples de l'Afrique*. Paris, La Découverte.

Sen, A., 1981. *Poverty and Famines: An Essay on Entitlements and Deprivation*. Oxford, Clarendon.

Sindjoun, L., 2002. *Sociologie des relations internationales*. Paris, Karthala.

Smouts, M.-C., 2001. *Forêts tropicales, jungle internationale*. Paris, Presses de Sciences Politiques.

Stockholm International Peace Research Institute, 2005. *Yearbook 2005. Armaments, Disarmament and International Security*. Stockholm.

Tabutin, D., 1994. *Population et sociétés en Afrique au sud du Sahara.* Paris, L'Harmattan.

Traoré, A., 2001. *L'étau: l'Afrique dans un monde sans frontières.* Arles, Actes Sud.

UNESCO, 1999. "La Traite esclavagiste, son histoire, sa mémoire, ses effets." *Cahiers des Anneaux de la mémoire,* no. 1. Nantes, Les Anneaux de la mémoire.

Von Braun, J., T. Teklu, and P. Webb, 1999. *Famines in Africa. Causes, Responses, and Prevention.* Washington D.C., International Food Policy Institute.

## Selected Internet Sites on Africa

*News*

www.africaonline.com: News about Africa (English)

www.african-geopolitics.org: Trimestrial review of news about Africa (English/French)

www.afrik.com: News about Africa

www.allafrica.com: Press review (English/French)

www.commissionforafrica.org: Report of the Commission for Africa (English)

*International Organizations*

www.oecd.org: Organization for Cooperation and Development

www.unctad.org: United Nations Conference on Trade and Development

www.undp.org: United Nations Development Program

www.unhcr.org: United Nations High Commissariat for Refugees

www.worldbank.org/afr: The World Bank's site on Africa

*Research Centers and NGOs*

www.amnesty.org: *Amnesty International*

www.cean.u-bordeaux.fr: Centre d'étude d'Afrique noire (CEAN), Institut d'études politiques (IEP) de Bordeaux (French)

www.crisisweb.org: International Crisis Group (ICG), an NGO
  specializing in the analysis of conflicts
www.democraf.com: Observatoire de la démocratie en Afrique
  (French)
www.hrw.org: *Human Rights Watch*

*Statistics*

www.europa.eu.int/comm/development: European Commission
  on Development
www.nepad.org: New Partnership for African Development

# INDEX

# About the Author and Translator

PHILIPPE HUGON is professor emeritus of economics at the University of Paris X Nanterre and director of the CERED/DET/FORUM (a center specializing in the economy of development and transition). He also directs the Program in Advanced Studies in the Economic Analysis of Development and is president of the Center for Studies and Research for a New Applied Economics (CERNEA). In addition, he is a consultant for numerous international and national organizations concerned with development aid (the World Bank, the International Labor Office, the European Commission, the Organization for Economic Co-operation and Development, the Ministry of Foreign Affairs, the United Nations Development Program, and UNESCO, and he was also a member of the High Council for International Cooperation (2000–2003).

Hugon is the author of over one hundred articles in specialized journals and more than fifteen books on international development and political economy, including *International Political Economy and Globalization* and, most recently, *The Economy of Africa.*

STEVEN RENDALL, the translator, is Professor Emeritus of Romance Languages at the University of Oregon and the author of numerous books and articles about French and European literature. He is also editor emeritus of *Comparative Literature.* He now lives in France and has translated thirty-eight books from French and German. Rendall has been the recipient of both the National Jewish Book Society's Sandra Brand and Arik Weintraub Award and the Modern Language Association's Scaglione Prize.